Golf in Columbus at Wyandot Country Club

A Lost Donald Ross Classic

WILLIAM R. CASE
Foreword by Kaye W. Kessler

Published by The History Press
Charleston, SC 29403
www.historypress.net

Copyright © 2014 by William R. Case
All rights reserved

First published 2014

ISBN 978-1-5402-1203-0

Library of Congress Control Number: 2014953166

Notice: The information in this book is true and complete to the best of our knowledge. It is offered without guarantee on the part of the author or The History Press. The author and The History Press disclaim all liability in connection with the use of this book.

All rights reserved. No part of this book may be reproduced or transmitted in any form whatsoever without prior written permission from the publisher except in the case of brief quotations embodied in critical articles and reviews.

To Lisa—she understands!

Contents

Foreword, by Kaye W. Kessler	7
Acknowledgements	11
Introduction	17

Part I: The Elks Years, 1922–31

1. The Founding Father	21
2. Pomp and Circumstance	27
3. The Great Man Arrives	33
4. "Play Away, Mr. Kaufman!"	40
5. Exploring the Lost Course	47
6. Denny Shute and the "Maker of Champions"	52
7. The Inventor	61
8. "Indian Bill"—The Last of the Wyandots	71
9. Fire Fork!	77

Part II: The Wyandot Years, 1931–46

10. Fire Sale!	85
11. Three Weeks	95
12. The End of a Great Elk	102
13. Ladies First	109
14. Fun Times	115
15. The Pro's Pro	123
16. Victory Gardens	131

Contents

Part III: The Municipal Course Years, 1946-52
   17. Reprieve!   141
   18. Showdown!   156
   19. Final Shots   166

Epilogue   173
Appendix. Memories of the Wyandot Golf Course,
   by Bill Amick   179
Index   181
About the Author   191

Foreword

Ah, if the old Elks/Wyandot Country Club could talk.

The what? The Elks/Wyandot Country Club. It was way up north, out in the country, above Clintonville, short of Worthington. Located right off old two-lane Morse Road, it was bordered on the east by the defunct CD&M trolley/railroad tracks and storied Indian Bill Moose's ramshackle hut, which drew more visitors on some Sundays than the Olentangy Amusement Park.

The what? Okay, so there aren't a thimbleful of Columbusites who have the vaguest idea. Try again with the Ohio Schools for the Deaf and Blind. Now you're with it—The Elks/Wyandot's wonderful eighteen holes are buried right under it (the Schools for the Deaf and Blind, not Olentangy Village). Play along—you'll love it. Yeah, I was there for the funeral.

The Elks/Wyandot had a convoluted, glorious and sadly short run of thirty years (1923–52)—some eighty-plus years back in another century. Bill Case knows it better than I or anybody in the continental United States, even though he never even saw the old course. That's why he wrote this wonderful book. He's sifted through the ashes so expertly, so perfectly that he's all but made Wyandot talk.

Bill's a retired litigation attorney who discovered Columbus in 1977 and took root. He and his wife, Lisa, are now infectious movers and shakers in the German Village Society. Just as noteworthy is the fact that Bill happens to be a Donald Ross disciple and a member of the Donald Ross Society, which more than revels in the over four hundred U.S. courses on

Foreword

which the revered architect (and most accomplished golfer himself) put his talented signature.

Ross designed and supervised construction of the late lamented Elks/Wyandot. His great work began when he did famed Pinehurst No. 2, site of the recent Men's and Women's U.S. Open, a doubleheader first. Ross all but created Pinehurst, also designing Nos. 1, 3 and 4. His fingerprints are all over courses in thirty-five states, with thirty-seven courses in Ohio, including Scioto Country Club, Columbus Country Club and long-departed Arlington, as well as nearby Granville, Zanesville, Athens Country Club and Toledo's Inverness. Ross's most celebrated designs include Seminole, Aronimink, Virginia's Homestead, the Broadmoor in Colorado, New Jersey's Plainfield Country Club, most of the Pines in Pinehurst—and The Elks/Wyandot.

Little wonder, then, that The Elks/Wyandot caught the eye and fascinated avid golfer and sportsman Case, who has done a riveting job of bringing Wyandot alive once again in this remarkable tome.

Bill relentlessly probed deep into the archives, pouring his heart and soul into the work and bringing the very cold facts to the surface one more time in a detailed but entertaining manner. He starts from the germ of an idea, when early day Columbus business tycoon John Kaufman purchased 265 acres in 1921 for the first-ever Elks (BPOE 37) golf course. He takes it through Ross's genius to a string of head pros from Lloyd Gullickson for openers to Hermon Shute, Francis Marzolf and Johnny Buchanan. Denny Shute (Hermon's son and one of my personal heroes) began his career at The Elks, and Bill will tell you what made this three-time major champion tick. The story winds through the desperate and debilitating Great Depression, the early 1930s transformation from The Elks to Wyandot Country Club and the hardships of World War II.

Bill left no fairway, ravine or rough unturned, weaving Columbus Country Club's legendary Charlie Lorms and Scioto's George Sargent into the theme. He also manages to introduce vignettes of Walter Hagen and Governor James Rhodes along with out-of-the-blue references to Presidents Warren Harding, FDR and HST; Bobby Jones; Gene Autry; Will Rogers; Bill "Bojangles" Robinson; Eddie Rickenbacker; and Generals Pershing Patten and MacArthur.

He devotes great attention to the excellence of greenkeeper Lawrence Huber and his family and the tragic autumn fire that made ashes of the clubhouse and changed the entire picture.

Hell, read it! Bill didn't miss a putt, skip the driver or leave anything in the bunkers. I wouldn't dream of tampering with his great labor of love.

Foreword

Besides, once the book was finished, Anglophiles Bill and Lisa took off for their semiannual excursions to the UK, doubtlessly making yet another pilgrimage to Ross's birthplace in Dornoch, Scotland.

If you hadn't guessed, I relished the resurrection of classic old Wyandot.

—Kaye W. Kessler

Acknowledgements

To quote a Beatles classic, this project quickly turned into a "Magical Mystery Tour." I witnessed that magic in action whenever I met with folks who shared their remembrances of old Wyandot. Talking about the old course invariably made them very happy, though at the same time a bit sad. My take was that it had been a long time since any of them had discussed the course and club in any detail, and tapping into their recollections served as a fond reminder of the important and positive role the course and club had played in their lives. Their sadness derives from the "Paradise Lost" caused by the closing of the course. It still hurts a little even sixty-two years later. The magic has left its imprint on me as well. I, like Shirley Edler, catch myself sometimes envisioning various holes at Wyandot and its forerunner, The Elks Country Club, though I never saw them firsthand. Like the Beatles song quoted above, there are still some "mysteries" concerning The Elks/Wyandot that might never be fully explained. The circumstances that led Harold Kaufman and his Glen Burn partners to sell the course to the State of Ohio in 1944 can only be surmised, not known for certain. And why didn't the city compete with the state to buy the golf course property when it had the chance? Did The Elks' unlucky clubhouse manager unwittingly do something that caused the spectacular fire that destroyed the clubhouse in 1930? Or was the cause faulty wiring?

The best way to present my heartfelt acknowledgements is to do so (more or less) in the order that they occurred—the same way I present the story. I got the idea for learning more about The Elks/Wyandot when Lisa and

Acknowledgements

I attended a meeting of the Donald Ross Society in September 2013 and perused a list prepared by the society of the courses designed by Ross. The list included "Elks Country Club—Worthington, Ohio, opened in 1923," a course of which I had never heard. The society works diligently to preserve Ross's classic courses. Had it been around in 1949, it would have thrown its collective weight behind Jim Rhodes's preservation efforts. Another entity that does much to preserve Donald Ross's heritage is the Tufts' Archives, located in Ross's home of Pinehurst, North Carolina. Audrey Moriarty, who directs that organization, has been an avid supporter of my research.

The first place I checked to find information about The Elks/Wyandot was the Internet. That is where I found Shirley Hyatt's wonderful Clintonville History blog. Shirley, already an accomplished author, helped me in a number of ways: assisting in setting up a lecturing opportunity for me on "The History of Golf in Clintonville," giving me tips on finding and working with a publisher and, most importantly, providing me a lead to finding Betty Huber, greenkeeper Lawrence Huber's daughter-in-law. Most of my key interviews emanated from Shirley's initially pointing me in Betty's direction.

Betty Huber, who still lives near where the course used to be, provided me with a treasure-trove of wonderful photos taken by Lawrence Huber during the construction of the course. She and her son Bill led me to Jim Huber, Lawrence's son, now residing in New Mexico. Jim, a retired air traffic controller, worked on green crews with his father at Brookside and University in his youth. Jim still enjoys the game and has built a full-scale golf hole on his property. Jim provided wonderful photographs of his father and the Columbus Invitational held at Wyandot in 1948.

Almost in passing, Jim recommended that I talk to his boyhood friend Bill Amick, the Florida golf architect. Bill, with his great eye for detail, had a nearly photographic memory of the holes. He, too, sent me photos and provided commentary after each chapter was published. I am delighted with his recollections of the course contained in the appendix. Bill recommended that I meet with Tom Marzolf, Francis Marzolf's grandson and also a preeminent golf architect. Tom provided many wonderful photos and stories. He told me to contact Ellen Marzolf Hallerman, Francis's daughter. She, in turn, generously forwarded great pictures and anecdotes as well. Tom also urged me to telephone Dow Finsterwald, one of the game's greats from 1955 to 1965 and winner of the 1958 PGA Championship. It was a thrill to talk to one of my childhood idols, and he couldn't have been nicer. At the suggestion of Gene Johnson and Bill Amick, I also met with renowned architect Mike Hurdzan Jr., whose father, Mike Sr., had been a

Acknowledgements

Wyandot member. Mike provided some wonderful Elks memorabilia from his unsurpassed collection. Thanks to Mike for giving me a private tour of what has to be the best private golf collection anywhere!

Another great source was Jim Thompson and his publication concerning Bill Moose, *The Last of the Wyandots*. "Indian Bill," who never played a round of golf in this life, was one of the course's most memorable characters.

The more I learned about The Elks/Wyandot, the more I began to envision that its tumultuous history might provide sufficient material for a book, not merely blog entries. I was struck by the impression that the course's ongoing battle for survival contained elements that might be found in an epic dramatic novel. My old running mate Chuck Ticknor was the first to spot this. When Brookside buddy Gene Johnson told me he was copying each chapter, I began to believe that my postings might be striking a chord with golf junkies at least. Another Brooksider, Kenny Galloway, echoed Gene's comments and performed some first-class editing as well. John Grant suggested I call Kaye Kessler, now living in Denver. What a great idea that was! Mr. Kessler sent me several e-mails recalling his experiences at Wyandot and with the Columbus Invitational. I am humbled by the fact that this nationally recognized hall-of-fame sportswriter agreed to ink the foreword to my book.

Once I learned that Dwight Watkins's father had been a member at Wyandot, and that Dwight himself had played and caddied there, I was forever pestering him for his recollections. His insights unlocked several doors for me in the course of the writing process. Dwight always took the time to correspond with me when one of my postings stirred his memory bank. Dr. Fred Balthaser and Dick Gordin, both well known in Columbus golf circles, also shared their recollections.

After I wrote the "The Pro's Pro" chapter, Joanie Armstrong Terango reached out to me and related her childhood experience of taking a golf lesson from Francis Marzolf. Joanie also had a good friend with whom she thought I might like to converse: Judith Florio, the daughter of one of the club's greatest players, Johnny Florio. Judith provided several artifacts, including a fantastic photograph of the final Wyandot "Old-Timers" reunion in 1950. Her loving remembrances brought colorful Johnny to life for me. Elaine Altmaier assisted with Kaufman family history.

Bill and Nancy Eisnaugle, while playing in Brookside's Opening Day couples event with Lisa and me, mentioned that their friend Shirley Edler had grown up playing old Wyandot. Shirley was a godsend, as I had been scratching around for material concerning the course's final days.

Acknowledgements

The fifteen-time Scioto club champion furnished rich anecdotes and wonderful photos of her times at the course. So did Sam Muldoon, another long-term Brooksider, with his whimsical tale concerning brother Bill Muldoon's obtaining a junior membership at Wyandot as a prize for winning a hole-in-one contest. The entertaining stories provided by Shirley and Sam made Chapter 19—"Last Shots"—one of my favorites. Having an opportunity to walk the old course was also enlightening. I did not find any old balls, but I had fun watching Dwight Watkins, Bill Amick and Shirley Edler stroke a few shots. Thanks to Bobbie Huebner of the Ohio School for the Deaf and Clint at the Ohio School for the Blind for letting us have the run of the campuses.

The "meat and potatoes" narrative came primarily from Columbus's three daily newspapers published during The Elks' and Wyandot's existence: the *Columbus Evening Dispatch*, the *Columbus Citizen* and the *Ohio State Journal*. It was definitely a stroke of good fortune to have three papers available for this research. If one of the papers did not have a story about a particular matter, there was a good chance one of the other two dailies would. I am forever grateful to Columbus's great old-school sportswriters like E.H. Peniston, Lathrop Mack, Lew Byrer, Bill Needham, Paul Hornung and Kaye Kessler, whose erudite columns and eyewitness accounts provided the basis for much of the content of this publication. Thanks to the ever-patient Jack Shaw and Gloria at the Columbus Metropolitan Library for taking the time to show me how to best use its fabulous resources. My morning coffee shop buddy Phil Sheridan was always spot-on with his grammatical corrections.

Curt Sampson, a nationally recognized author of numerous golf history books and who grew up with me in Hudson, Ohio, once remarked that I was capable of writing something like this. I am grateful to him for planting that suggestion. Curt, sorry it took me ten years to make it happen! Other writers like Terese Houle and my daughter Hadley Henriette encouraged me in myriad ways during the entire process. So did Jan Hanson, Linda and Bob Harbrecht, Bruce Savage, John Terango, Anne Eckhart, Ron Geese, Steve Wiley, Anne Eckhart, Dave Royer, Dan Strasser, Mike Detjen, John Mazza, Art and Carol Norman, Ritchey and Becki Hollenbaugh, Bob Barnett, Rick VanBrimmer and three lifetime friends from my Hudson days: Dan MacLellan, Tim Weidman and Ann Russell. Mary Rogers and the Clintonville Historical Society afforded me an opportunity to speak about The Elks/Wyandot recently. The positive feedback from that experience was most gratifying and kept me moving forward to compose the remainder of the story. I also appreciate Marilyn Strasser's sharing of her recollections of

Acknowledgements

Lawrence Huber and the Huber family. A special thanks goes to John Stiles of the Donald Ross Society for his encouragement and support.

Mammoth technical support has come from Teddy Hammond, Melissa Richwine and John Clark. I could not have done any of this without their hardworking efforts on my behalf.

I have enjoyed working with The History Press and editors Greg Dumais and Will Collicott. They have given a fledging author a chance, and the opportunity is greatly appreciated.

My legal training was more useful than I anticipated in this project. Sequencing the telling of the story in an orderly manner was critical here, and I was taught how to do that in preparing legal briefs by mentors George McConnaughey, Bill Moul and Bob Mone.

I did a smart thing in the course of researching and writing this golf course story—I adopted every suggestion offered by my wonderful wife, Lisa Case. Her instincts on such matters are unerring. I know at times she was exasperated with my obsession for telling the story of this old abandoned course, but she was patient and understanding throughout. She has a very probing and critical eye, and she likes the story. That is good enough for me!

Introduction

Central Ohio golfers never tire debating the relative merits of the many great courses in the area. Jack Nicklaus's Muirfield, Scioto, University Scarlet, Double Eagle, The Golf Club, Brookside, Columbus, The Lakes and Champions have their devotees. But players who had the good fortune to strike their brassies over the long-vanished course first known as The Elks Country Club and later as Wyandot Country Club could argue with some justification that this Donald Ross–designed beauty was the finest of all.

From its ballyhooed opening in 1923 until its sad and final closing after the 1952 golf season, the course—and the country clubs associated with it (Elks and Wyandot)—faced daunting challenges. While the course overcame the hardships of the Great Depression, a disastrous fire that burned the clubhouse to the ground and World War II, it ultimately could not survive a political struggle with the State of Ohio, despite the best efforts of Columbus mayor (and later four-time governor of Ohio) Jim Rhodes to save it.

My interest in the history of The Elks/Wyandot was sparked when I discovered errors in the Donald Ross Society's (I am a member) list of his designs. First, it stated that "Elks Country Club," constructed in 1923 in Worthington, Ohio (a Columbus suburb), was still in existence. I knew that there was no longer any course by that name in central Ohio. Second, the list identified "Wyandot Golf Course" in Centerburg (another suburb much farther away) as a Ross course that was opened in 1922 and closed in 1952. Ross could not have served as architect for this little country course since it

Introduction

opened after I moved to Columbus in the '70s—decades after Ross's death. Moreover, that course is still in operation.

So this misinformation piqued my curiosity, and I embarked on what can best be described as a "research adventure." In short order, I confirmed some basic facts. The Benevolent and Protective Order of Elks, Columbus Lodge No. 37 (BPOE) acquired 265 acres of property bordering on Morse Road and Indianola Avenue in the Clintonville area of Columbus in 1921. The Elks then retained famed architect Donald Ross to design a golf course on the property, which was opened for play in 1923. "The Elks Country Club" owned and operated these facilities until 1931, when the course name changed to "Wyandot Country Club." The course closed for good in 1952. The facilities of the Ohio School for the Deaf now occupy the area where The Elks and Wyandot clubhouses once stood. The School for the Deaf is accessible from Morse Road over roughly the same driveway that was used to access the clubhouses many years ago. The Ohio School for the Blind occupies the northwest portion of the property across a deep and forested ravine that effectively separates its campus from that of its sister school. The School for the Blind is accessible from High Street, which is Columbus's principal north–south artery.

But I wanted to know more. What led the Elks to acquire this large property and build a golf course? Was Donald Ross on site (he often did not see courses he designed)? Could any information about the course layout or details about Ross's bunkering be obtained? Why did the club name change to Wyandot? Did the Elks sell out—and if so, why? How good was the golf course? Did players of distinction in local circles play their golf there? Is anyone alive who can remember the course, let alone have played it? What were the circumstances that led to its ultimate closing and acquisition by the state?

I was able to answer these questions. I pieced together the history of the course by spending many hours buried in the microfilm archives of Columbus newspapers. I walked the property and found remnants of the old course. Internet searches unearthed many informative tidbits concerning the club's founders, members and staff that helped flesh out the story. I acquired a program for a PGA tour event played at Wyandot in 1948—the Columbus Invitational. A visit to the county courthouse uncovered a 1938 aerial photo of the course, which revealed much about Ross's routing, as well as many of his architectural details. Most gratifying of all was my opportunity to reminisce with folks who were of a certain age that they could recall the old course and relate anecdotes about the people associated with it. This resulted in uncovering treasure-troves of photographs and other artifacts, many of which are viewable in these pages. Now, let me tell you the story of The Elks/Wyandot.

PART I

The Elks Years,
1922–31

Chapter 1
THE FOUNDING FATHER

To label John W. Kaufman merely an entrepreneur would do him an injustice. He was much more. From approximately 1900 until his death in 1933, he was a colossus of Columbus's burgeoning business community. Mr. Kaufman was responsible for founding or acquiring an array of quarrying and manufacturing operations that mushroomed into major-league enterprises. He embodied the Horatio Alger "rags to riches" success story that inspired youths of the era.

His career began juggling two low-level jobs. During the day, he clerked for the Reinhard Bank in downtown Columbus. He moonlighted as an assistant bookkeeper for the Godman Shoe Company. He impressed the latter employer well enough that he was steadily promoted through the ranks until he became the firm's part owner and secretary. After reaching age forty in 1906, Mr. Kaufman upped his entrepreneurial activities. Anticipating that the city was about to embark on a growth spurt that would necessitate an increased need for building materials, he and several of his siblings purchased the Woodruff and Pausch Company, a limestone mining operation adjacent to the Scioto River on Columbus's northwest side. The investment went well, and in short order, the Kaufman interests also swallowed up the Casparis Stone Company. The resulting merged company became known as the Marble Cliff Quarry Co., a vast operation covering over two thousand acres. And Mr. Kaufman proved to be spot-on in his assessment that Columbus would need his product. Limestone mined from the quarry was used in the construction of Ohio Stadium, the forty-seven-story American Insurance

Golf in Columbus at Wyandot Country Club

John W. Kaufman. *Columbus Memory, Scripps-Howard Newspapers/Grandview Heights Public Library/photo.org Collection.*

Union Citadel (now the LeVeque Tower), the city airport and area freeways. In time, the Kaufmans, with John leading the family's efforts, acquired many other mines and quarrying operations in the United States and Canada.

Most would have been content with such success, but resting on his laurels was not in John Kaufman's makeup. He and other family members launched investments in Claycraft Brick & Mining Company, the Arrow Sand and Gravel Company in Columbus and the Ohio Steel Foundry in Lima. He was in on the ground floor of Columbus Coated Fabrics, which became the industry leader in the manufacture of vinyl-coated cloth products. Given Mr. Kaufman's far-flung business interests, it would have been understandable if he had begged off from participating in civic endeavors. But as the saying goes, "If you want a job done, give it to a busy person!" And John Kaufman was always there to lend a hand. He raised enormous funds for the World War I "war chest drive" and supported Charity Newsies, a local charity still providing clothing to underprivileged children. With his wife, Elizabeth, and their three children, he found time to be a "hale fellow well-met" socially as well. Kaufman's memberships at Scioto and Columbus Country Clubs, as well as the Columbus Club and Athletic Club of Columbus, evidenced this.

But aside from work and family, John Kaufman's chief passion was the BPOE—the Elks. While membership has dwindled in recent decades, Elks lodges in John Kaufman's time served as many communities' social organization of choice. It should be remembered that this was the

The Elks Years, 1922–31

nascent stage of private country clubs in America, and they were not yet a competitive threat to fraternal organizations such as the Elks. So the BPOE thrived. It counted among its members Presidents Harding, Franklin Roosevelt, Truman and, later, Kennedy and Ford. Military heroes were drawn to the BPOE as well. Generals Pershing, Patton and MacArthur and Columbus's own World War I flying ace Captain Eddie Rickenbacker joined. So did Bobby Jones, Gene Autry, Buffalo Bill Cody, Will Rogers and Bill "Bojangles" Robinson.

The BPOE could not have had a more devoted member and booster than John Kaufman. His talent for recruitment of new members received mention in the 1913 edition of the trade publication *American Clay Magazine*, in which it was noted, "If John Kaufman is as good a clay booster as he is an Elks booster, the sales ledger of the Claycraft Brick & Mining Company of Columbus, Ohio will show an increase each season. Recently Mr. Kaufman interested his relatives in the Elks' lodge, and eight of them joined at one time. Mr. Kaufman is president of the brick company."

When the BPOE decided to move its lodge from Main Street, Mr. Kaufman headed up the building committee charged with finding new quarters. An imposing new Frank Packard–designed lodge home at 256 East Broad Street was dedicated in 1915. John Kaufman was rewarded

Elks Lodge No. 37, 256 East Broad Street, built and dedicated in 1915. *Columbus Memory, Scripps-Howard Newspapers/Grandview Heights Public Library/photo.org Collection.*

for his unstinting efforts on behalf of Columbus Elks Lodge No. 37 by elevation to its leader (in Elks parlance, the "Grand Exulted Ruler") in 1918.

Aside from the fact that America was involved in a war, it is hard to imagine that the life of fifty-two-year-old John Kaufman could have been much better in 1918. He resided in a beautiful mansion with his family at the then-posh address of 1151 Bryden Road. Offices for his far-flung businesses were only minutes away from home. Wartime needs necessitated high demand for the products of several of his enterprises. He had achieved the leadership of his beloved Elks, and Lodge No. 37 was less than a five-minute drive away. He had built a business empire that supported many of his many siblings and their families (John was one of ten children), and twenty-eight-year-old son Harold was really coming along in assisting with the management of Marble Cliff's operations.

But John Kaufman was not satisfied with the status quo. With the arrival of Columbus, Scioto and Aladdin Country Clubs on the local scene, he realized that golf was the rising sport, and country clubs would be needed to meet the demand. No doubt he thought, "Why shouldn't my Elks have their own country club?" Mr. Kaufman might have been influenced by the fact that the Shriners were already taking steps to expand their Aladdin Country Club course to eighteen holes in nearby Upper Arlington. Another local fraternal organization, the York Masonic Lodge, was also entertaining the same notion and several years later would open York Temple Country Club.

Whatever the converging motivating factors that led to Kaufman's dream, he must have realized immediately that he had discovered the perfect land for a country club after laying eyes on the one-hundred-acre estate owned by wholesale grocer Charles Higgins in present-day Clintonville. This now highly developed area of Columbus still qualified as rural when Kaufman first got wind of it—probably in 1920. As was described in the *Ohio State Journal*, seventy-five acres of the Higgins property "are level and beautified by every device of the modern landscape gardener. The other 25 acres are hilly and heavily wooded. The principal building on the property is an 18-room house [then only eleven years old] with six bathrooms. There are also a seven-room house for the caretaker, barns for horses, cattle, and farm machinery, power house and a large greenhouse." Moreover, given that the estate rested in the hands of bankers who had formed a creditors' committee for Mr. Higgins, it seemed likely that Kaufman could acquire the property for a reasonable price.

The Elks Years, 1922-31

The Elks' country home, the former Charles Higgins estate. *Betty Huber collection.*

This scenario is akin to what confronted Bobby Jones when he first eyed Fruitlands Nursery some thirteen years later. The owner of that incomparable property was likewise looking to liquidate an estate. The nursery's grounds similarly boasted impeccable landscaping, as well as a beautiful home that could seamlessly transition into use as a clubhouse. Jones saw at once that the property would make for an ideal golf course. That abandoned nursery became Augusta National Golf Club.

Golf in Columbus at Wyandot Country Club

The only problem with the Higgins property was that it was not large enough for an eighteen-hole golf course. Nine maybe, but no more! But Kaufman learned that there were three adjoining undeveloped properties across the wide, wooded ravine totaling another 165 acres, which, if added to the Higgins land, would be more than enough property to build a course that the Elks would be proud of.

Chapter 2
POMP AND CIRCUMSTANCE

The spring of 1921 found the members of Elks Lodge No. 37 in an uproar. Rumors were rampant that the lodge's now "Past Exulted Ruler," John W. Kaufman, was scheming to start a country club for the members and was negotiating to buy land on Columbus's north side expressly for that purpose. But Mr. Kaufman stayed close-mouthed about his plans, keeping only the other lodge officers in the loop. There was good cause for keeping things close to the vest. While Kaufman felt certain he could obtain the one-hundred-acre Higgins farm (complete with the house's silverware and china and the farm's livestock and thoroughbred chickens), he knew the fledgling country club would eventually have need of four other adjoining parcels, all owned by different individuals, in order to feature an eighteen-hole golf course. It would figure that Kaufman did not want the owners of these four parcels to be tipped off that their land was indispensable to that goal. So, when he announced to the surprised and pleased Elks members in late April that he was arranging to purchase the Higgins estate and convert it into a country club for the BPOE, Kaufman soft-pedaled things by leaving the impression that the BPOE would have all the land it needed with that purchase alone. The press was informed that the Higgins farm was sufficient for the Elks' purposes since "there was room for a nine-hole golf course, tennis courts, and a baseball diamond."

Seizing on its opportunity to publicize this new country home of the Elks, the BPOE scheduled a dedication ceremony at the property for May 28, 1921. By that time, the Higgins transfer was accomplished, and Kaufman had inked an agreement for the BPOE to buy the critical sixty-four-acre Smith property. Acquisitions of the thirty-one-acre Dell and thirteen-acre Fink parcels were not concluded until July 23. Finally, the BPOE would have enough land to construct eighteen holes! The final piece of the country club puzzle, the forty-six-acre Samples property, was not in the BPOE's hands until April 22, 1922.

While Kaufman busied himself in mid-May with the various details of getting The Elks Country Club off the ground, golf's most renowned architect was working just a few miles away. The Aladdin Country Club had engaged Donald Ross to stake out a redesign and expansion of its existing nine-hole course. Aladdin, a Ross gem now lost to the sands of time, was located at First Avenue and Arlington Avenue in the Upper Arlington/Grandview area of town. Ross expressed confidence that Aladdin "would be a splendid test of golf when completed" and that "on no hole will it be necessary to play over a railroad or traction tracks, which at present intercept four fairways in the nine holes now in use." Ross was feted at a dinner at Aladdin the night of May 16. Since this visit was noted by the *Ohio State Journal*, Kaufman certainly got wind that the architect was in town. Less than one year later, Ross would return to Columbus to work on Kaufman's project.

The dedication of the property was front-page news in all three of Columbus's daily newspapers. It was duly noted in the *Sunday Dispatch* that Elks Lodge No. 37 was the first in the country to "acquire a country club as an adjunct to the regular lodge home." The ceremony was staged on the lawn surrounding a new flagpole in the center of what was described as an "outdoor lodge room" specially prepared for the event. Kaufman called on former governor and fellow Elk James Campbell to address the assembled throng of over three hundred. Resplendent in his white suit, Campbell complimented the local lodge on its civic involvement in Columbus. He paid kind tributes to the work of Mr. Kaufman and his committee in securing the Higgins estate. Elks dedication rituals followed. The keys to the new "country home" of the lodge were presented to John Kaufman, who made a brief but heartfelt address. The *Ohio State Journal* mentioned that a "social air was given to the performance by the presence of more than 100 women, who appeared in summery dresses and added color to the scene."

Then the big moment arrived. Master John Altmaier, the four-year-old grandson of John Kaufman, was entrusted with the task of raising the new club's immense American flag up the flagpole. The *Journal*, with the hyper-drama typical of newspaper accounts of the time, reported, "A shaft of golden sunlight, breaking through a heavy cloud, shimmered on

THE ELKS YEARS, 1922–31

Former governor James Campbell addresses the BPOE at the dedication of the Elks' new "country home." *From the* Ohio State Journal, *May 29, 1921.*

the American flag as it rose to the top of the flag pole...The Elks' chorus broke into the strains of 'The Star Spangled Banner' as 200 Elks uncovered and saluted the flapping banner. There was silence, and then an outburst of applause...It was during the flag-raising that the assembled Elks first experienced the 'at-home' feeling."

Young Master Altmaier's picture graced the front page of the *Sunday Dispatch* just under the header. Outside of a royal baby, the four-year-old had to rank as one of the youngest lads ever to land on page one. As I viewed this archive, it occurred to me that there was at least a remote possibility that John Altmaier might still be alive, albeit well into his nineties. Wouldn't it be cool to interview someone who figured in an event that occurred ninety-two years ago? So I Googled the name "John Altmaier" in Columbus. I was blown away when the search came back with information indicating the presence of a gentleman by that name, age ninety-six, purportedly residing on Brookside Drive in the Columbus suburb of Bexley! Telephone inquiries were unavailing, so I wound up knocking on the door at the address provided by my Internet surfing. A kindly lady answered the door. I asked if John Altmaier still lived there. She smiled and replied that Mr. Altmaier had passed away twenty years previously. John's widow, Elaine, was still very much alive; however, she was away, summering in the Upper Peninsula.

The lady was nice enough to provide Elaine Altmaier's telephone number, and I called her. She was very sharp. Elaine confirmed that her deceased husband was indeed the grandson of John W. Kaufman. When I asked her about John's front-page picture on the May 29, 1921 *Sunday Dispatch*, she laughed and indicated that John never once mentioned it to her in their long marriage. Given his tender years at the time, he might never have been made aware of the picture or his role in the dedication ceremony. I asked if her husband ever became an Elk or played golf at The Elks/Wyandot. She replied that he did not. "John was a tennis player!" she said. While she could not tell me much about The Elks/Wyandot, Elaine provided very helpful information regarding the Kaufman business interests. Her late husband was employed with the Columbus Coated Fabrics portion of the family conglomerate, having risen to the vice-presidency of that company.

By the time of the dedication, Kaufman, in consultation with the new Grand Exulted Ruler of Elks Lodge No. 37, William Abbott, had determined that John R. Downey would serve as manager of both its city and country houses. In short order, Downey found the man he thought had the stuff to be a good greenkeeper (not "greenskeeper" because the entire course, not just the eighteen greens, must be kept

The Elks Years, 1922-31

The greenkeeper's home. *Betty Huber collection.*

"green") despite his lack of experience in the area. There was only one problem: Lawrence Huber was unmarried, although he was smitten with young Eunice whom he squired about in the small town of Alton, just west of Columbus. In the interview, Downey advised Lawrence in no uncertain terms that the BPOE wanted a married man to be living in the caretaker's home adjacent to the planned course. That would eliminate gossip concerns, etc.

Lawrence probably took all of five seconds to respond, "No problem—Eunice and I will get married right away!" And so they did. The Elks had found its greenkeeper. Lawrence Huber would be the one constant at The Elks/Wyandot for the next twenty years.

But the BPOE still needed to design and build its golf course. John Kaufman wanted the best. That could only mean the firm of Donald J. Ross and Associates and its eponymous founder. It is a fact that there are numerous Ross designs upon which the architect never set foot, working instead from his office in Pinehurst, North Carolina, by formulating his blueprints from topographical drawings. Presumably, if you wanted the great man to stake the course personally, you paid a little extra. But John W. perceived that Ross's presence on site would be well worth the added expense. Besides, the Shriners had engaged Ross to personally stake their Aladdin course. Kaufman's Elks were not about to take a backseat to any social organization in town!

Ross would have traveled north from Pinehurst to Columbus by train. It certainly had to be a nervous and excited Elks welcoming party that met Ross at the Union Station platform on April 27, 1922. Many thoughts had to be going through the greeters' respective minds. What would Ross think of the property's suitability for a golf course? Was he going to utilize the land's picturesque, wooded ravine for some of the holes? Or was the ravine too wide?

Chapter 3

THE GREAT MAN ARRIVES

It is fair to assume that by the time the industrialist and the course architect drove past the turreted edifice marking the rear entrance to the Elks' new country home, they had already bonded. John W. Kaufman and Donald Ross possessed traits and experiences that each man would have admired in the other. Both exhibited a capacity for risk taking—Kaufman by virtue of his gutsy and hugely successful acquisition of quarrying operations, and Ross by forsaking his comfortable position as the Tom Morris–trained golf professional at Dornoch, Scotland, and emigrating to the United States in 1899 to seek his fortune. Both derived their living from the land—John W. extracted stone from it; Ross reshaped it. Neither rested on his laurels after initial business success. Ross capitalized on the favorable reviews he received for his work on the Pinehurst courses for James Tufts by expanding his design activities up and down the eastern seaboard. Kaufman parlayed his Marble Cliff Quarries success into an empire by purchasing more mines and other vertically integrated operations.

Mr. Ross enjoyed traveling and would have appreciated Kaufman's wanderlust. The Columbus native frequently toured what was still the "Wild West," eventually writing a remarkable book about his extended western camping trip with five fellow Elks in 1925. Both Ross and Kaufman were amiable enough, but after the obligatory pleasantries, it would have been their mutual mindset to attend to the business at hand.

Kaufman would have marveled at Ross's often-overlooked skill as a golfer. He was one of the game's most accomplished players from 1900 to 1910.

Will Lay Out Elks' Golf Course

Donald Ross's arrival at The Elks was trumpeted by the *Ohio State Journal*. From the *Ohio State Journal, April 27, 1922*.

During that span, Ross won the Massachusetts Open twice and the prestigious North and South Open (played at his home of Pinehurst) three times. He recorded five top-ten finishes in the U.S. Open (the same number as Greg Norman). One of the few players compiling a better record during this stretch was Donald's brother Alex Ross, a six-time champion at the Massachusetts Open as well as the North and South. Alex is best remembered for winning the 1907

The Elks Years, 1922–31

U.S. Open at the Philadelphia Cricket Club with a tally of 302—10 better than his big brother Donald, who finished tenth. In 1910, Donald made a sentimental visit to his ancestral home, during which he made a surprising run in the Open Championship at St. Andrews. He finished a strong T8 behind winner and fellow outstanding UK golf architect James Braid. Thereafter, Ross began phasing out of competitive golf to concentrate full time on his course design work.

Stenograph of Donald Ross, a top-flight player, in action. *Library of Congress.*

During the next decade, Ross cemented his reputation as golf's preeminent designer with architectural triumphs at Oakland Hills, Scioto, Plainfield and Inverness. At the time he arrived in Columbus in April 1922 to start work on the Elks' property, Ross was in the midst of the most productive period of his long career, as he designed twenty-four new courses in 1922. He was particularly busy that season in central Ohio. In addition to commencing the Elks project and finalizing Aladdin, Ross was also designing Delaware Country Club (aka Odovene Country Club) and Springfield. He would be retained to lay out the Granville Golf Course in 1923.

Upon arrival, Ross and Kaufman met with the Elks' golf committee, composed of Harold Kaufman, Arthur Shannon and T.V. Taylor. Often when Ross staked a course, the clubhouse had yet to be built. In those cases, he would sometimes provide input as to where it should be located. Here, the country house was already in place. Ross saw immediately that its placement would be perfect relative to where he envisioned the routing for the starting and finishing holes for each of the nines. He spent the day walking the property, setting stakes here and there. By twilight, Mr. Ross had the tentative routing "well in mind." Better yet, he expressed delight with the scenic canvas with which he was working. "It's a beautiful spot, isn't it?" exclaimed the architect appreciatively to *Ohio State Journal* reporter E.H. Peniston in an interview late in the day.

The committee had wondered how Ross would deal with the deep, wooded ravine that divided the property. There might have been sentiment to locate a

Donald Ross, America's greatest golf course architect. *The Tufts Archives*.

green site or two in its valley to take full advantage of the terrain's natural beauty. But Ross rejected that idea because there was "so much wash there during the rainy seasons as to make good greens impracticable." Moreover, the ravine was, in his judgment, too wide in most places to be utilized. Thus, the ravine would be crossed only twice. However, Ross still found a way to take strategic advantage of the ravine, by using its heavily wooded slopes to shape sharp doglegs on several holes. In keeping with his philosophy of

The Elks Years, 1922-31

using the ground as he found it to the extent possible, Ross did not see the need to cut down many trees. The architect also observed that maintenance of the course would be enhanced by the presence of the woods because its "carpet of leaf mold will be a real benefit to the greens of the course...since it will furnish the best top dressing and make for the best of greens." Ross knew what he was doing, as the well-conditioned greens would be a hallmark of the course throughout its existence. He promised that the Elks would have a "fine course" and a "good test of golf" with "well systematized trapping and raised greens," an ever-present staple in Ross's designs.

Ross was on site at The Elks from Thursday, April 27, until Monday, May 1. Watching Ross closely was greenkeeper Lawrence Huber, who would have the task of assisting the golf committee with the course's construction. Years later, Huber told his son Jim how much he admired Ross's attention to detail. Every stake was set with an eye for how the land would drain in that particular location. Ross's tiling to eliminate moisture collection areas in the fairways impressed Lawrence as well. Appropriate drainage was something Huber was attuned to from his experience farming in Jackson County before moving to Columbus.

The third hole, a 179-yard par three. *Betty Huber collection.*

Golf in Columbus at Wyandot Country Club

Ross boarded the train back to Pinehurst on Monday. Working from his cottage bordering the third hole of his beloved Pinehurst No. 2, he prepared the blueprints with dispatch and then promptly forwarded them to Harold Kaufman and the other committee members. Construction and seeding was underway by late spring. The course began to take shape late in the year, as photographs taken by Lawrence Huber demonstrate.

On the third hole, Ross fashioned what appears to have elements of a "Redan" hole (the term "Redan" is derived from a military fortification set at a V-shaped salient angle toward an expected attack). The green was well protected by a yawning bunker to the right and a heavy slope to the left, running diagonally with the right front portion of the green closest to the tee. The original Redan hole—the fifteenth at North Berwick, Scotland—was imitated by Charles Blair MacDonald and other early American golf architects. However, it should be noted that Ross is on record as not favoring Redan holes. In any event, it is clearly evident from this photograph that Ross was making good on his pledge to build raised and well-protected greens.

This photo of the picturesque fourteenth hole was taken by Lawrence Huber in the early days of construction. *Betty Huber collection.*

The Elks Years, 1922–31

If The Elks Country Club had designated a "signature hole," it would have been the picturesque 137-yard, par-three fourteenth. Ross was not a fan of having an over-abundance of water holes. But if there were an attractive pond located on a property, he would often bring it into play on a short par three. The view from the hole's elevated tee was glorious. A niblick shot cleanly hit would safely carry the intervening hazard. However, even in these early stages of construction, it is apparent that the shot had better be on the money, or disaster would loom. The fourteenth green was the sole exception to Ross's initial preference not to locate a green in the ravine. The view was just too good to pass up.

By the spring of 1923, everything was on schedule. Once the seeding had taken hold, the course would be ready for play. Elks members waited impatiently through May for its opening. Finally, John W. decreed that the course's opening day ceremony would take place on Saturday, June 16. Given the spectacular country home dedication two years before, there was rampant speculation as to what sort of show John W. would unveil this time. Would there be a match scheduled of top professionals? Would there be a tee shot hit off the number-one tee to commemorate the opening—and if so, who would do the honors?

Chapter 4
"PLAY AWAY, MR. KAUFMAN!"

Saturday, June 16, 1923, was a great day to be a member of the BPOE, Columbus Lodge No. 37. The long-awaited unveiling of the lodge's new Donald Ross–designed golf course was now a reality. The course would be the first anywhere to be owned and operated by a BPOE lodge. Two Elks in particular—John W. Kaufman and his thirty-three-year-old son, Harold—must have been really keyed up . For John W., the ceremony marked the crowning achievement of several years of tireless effort on behalf of Lodge No. 37. His service as chair of the lodge's building committee had resulted in the acquisition of its magnificent downtown home. He had found the land and buildings for the lodge's "country home," arranged for their purchase and hired the greatest architect in the land to design a championship golf course on the grounds. John W. was a proud man, and he no doubt viewed it as a matter of import that his course be favorably received by fellow Elks and Columbus's golf community.

As Saturday morning approached, Harold had his own reasons for being anxious. As chair of the golf committee, he had been entrusted with the responsibility of making sure that Donald Ross's blueprints were followed and that the course was ready for play by its scheduled debut. But poor spring weather had interfered with the progress of putting the course into top shape. There was only so much that the committee and greenkeeper Lawrence Huber could do. The greens, though growing in satisfactorily, were bumpy, and the fairway grass was still a little soft and spotty in a few places. The course would simply not be at its best by Saturday's festivities. Harold could only hope that the onlookers would understand the reasons

The Elks Years, 1922–31

for the course's lack of conditioning and would focus instead on its beauty and Donald Ross's impeccable routing of the holes. As E.H. Peniston of the *Ohio State Journal* noted in his article the day following the opening ceremony, "There are carries over ravines, many bits of woods to lose shots on, brooks and a lake to plunge into, and many well-placed traps."

But there was another reason why Harold might have lost sleep in advance of June 16. It had been determined that by virtue of his hard work as chair of the committee, he should be accorded the honor of opening the course by hitting the very first drive on hole number one. There would be a big crowd eyeballing that inaugural drive, and Harold wanted it to be a good one.

There was a third man who wanted very much to make a good impression that Saturday—newly appointed golf professional Lloyd Gullickson. Most of the Elks would be getting their first look at the young, strapping Illinois native. They had heard he was a pretty fair player. Young Lloyd had won honors as golf champion of the navy in 1918. After he was discharged, he made a surprising run in the 1922 U.S. Open at Skokie Country Club, outside Chicago. After a sterling 70 in the tournament's second round placed him only five back, it seemed Lloyd stood a realistic chance. He faded thereafter but still finished a respectable T28, losing out to rising star twenty-year-old Gene Sarazen. The payoff for competing in the major championships was not prize money (Sarazen's first prize at Skokie was $500; Gullickson's fine showing earned him nothing). What really mattered was that a good finish in a major championship would bring recognition that could help struggling young pros like Lloyd land a steady club professional job. His strong Open performance certainly helped his cause in becoming the first Elks' pro. To commemorate the opening, three other local pros would be joining Gullickson in a four-ball exhibition match. While Lloyd was used to high-level competition, he nevertheless would be feeling some pressure to give a good account of himself in front of the BPOE golfers with whom he would be dealing in his new job.

Saturday's proceedings commenced with the dignitaries marching to enthusiastic applause from the locker house facility (which was "a model for completeness of accommodations," according to E.H. Peniston) to the dais fronting the country house. Then, Old Glory was raised to the top of the flagpole by Master Richard "Dick" Royer Price, the son of Lodge No. 37's Past Exalted Ruler. In the photo below, young Dick appears to be around four years old—the same age as John Altmaier when he had performed the flag-raising honors two years before at the country home dedication. Perhaps young Master Altmaier, now a doddering six-year-old, was considered too long in the tooth to reprise his role!

Golf in Columbus at Wyandot Country Club

Master Richard "Dick" Royer Price raising the flag at the course's dedication. *From the* Ohio State Journal, *June 17, 1923.*

Mr. Price, as master of ceremonies, then called on John W. Kaufman, the man without whose efforts the course—"the first in the history of Elkdom in the U.S."—would never have become a reality. John W., in keeping with Elks tradition, "presented the club" to Lodge No. 37's most current Grand Exalted Ruler, Robert Beatty. Columbus mayor James Thomas, lending some political punch to the occasion, praised the lodge and the Kaufmans for their tremendous achievement. Finally, Harold Kaufman rose to address the throng. It did not go unnoticed that a changing of the guard between father and son Kaufman seemed to be taking place. John W. had already ceded day-to-day control of Marble Cliff Quarries to Harold. Now, Harold was front and center on the golf committee and making what amounted to the valedictorian address of the ceremony. Harold expressed confidence that the course would develop into a "splendid" one and further remarked that its availability would add to the already broad range of activities of the local lodge.

Then something happened that Harold was not expecting. In tribute to his unstinting efforts in leading the golf committee through the construction phase, the BPOE bestowed on him a lifetime membership with the accompanying document packaged in a gold case. On the heels of this surprise, Harold had to gather himself and focus on his next task of striking the opening blow off the first tee. Sporting fashionable plus fours, the bespectacled Harold carefully teed a ball painted with Elks' colors of purple and white and took aim. To his relief and the crowd's delight, he struck a beauty "across a treacherous gulley and

The Elks Years, 1922-31

Top left shows Harold Kaufman's opening drive; top center shows part of the opening ceremony in front of the clubhouse; top right is Mayor James Thomas making his address; bottom left is John W. Kaufman presenting the course to the lodge; bottom right is the new locker house with caddies ready to go. *From the* Ohio State Journal, *June 17, 1923.*

straight up the first fairway." Though the photograph of the drive was snapped over ninety years ago, Harold's well-balanced follow-through would evidence a good shot both then and now.

Harold's tee ball was followed by drives of three other golfers who comprised the first foursome. Two of them were Arthur Shannon and T.V. Taylor, who served with Harold on the golf committee. Rounding out the first group to play the course was the event's honorary guest, W.O. Henderson, identified by the daily newspapers as "the dean of Columbus golfers."

Once the inaugural group was out of range, the spectators waited with anticipation for the main event—a four-ball match of local professionals featuring new pro Gullickson, the first professional at The Elks Country Club. However, one of Lloyd's opponents was no ordinary club pro. Scioto's professional, George Sargent, had long been recognized as one of the game's finest players. An Englishman by birth, Sargent had shown natural aptitude for the game when, at age nineteen, he finished T-31 in the 1901 British Open at St. Andrews. He then immigrated to Canada, where he became the pro at Royal Ottawa Golf Club. He found his way to another club job in Vermont and then entered the 1909 U.S. Open at Englewood Golf Club in New Jersey. Playing steadily, he hung close to the lead through three rounds. A sterling 71 on the final brought him home clear by four shots over Tim McNamara. Sargent's total of 290 was a new Open record. He received $300 prize money. While he never repeated as champion, George was a consistent threat to win the U.S. Open for the next seven years. His finishes starting in 1910 and ending in 1916 were: T16, T7, 6, T21, T3, T10 and T4. Once he became Scioto's first pro (and revolutionized golf instruction by being the first to use motion pictures to analyze the golf swing), Sargent appeared infrequently in tournaments. However, he still had enough game to finish T29 at the U.S. Open less than a month after the exhibition at The Elks.

Lloyd Gullickson knew Sargent and four-ball partner Herb Vallette of Winding Hollow would make for formidable opponents. But he was comforted by the knowledge that Charlie Lorms was to be his partner.

George Sargent, 1909 U.S. Open champion and professional at Scioto Country Club. *Library of Congress.*

The Elks Years, 1922-31

Lorms had recently moved south from Toledo, where he had served as pro for three years at Inverness, a fabulous Ross course that had hosted the 1920 U.S. Open. No doubt it occurred to Gullickson that Lorms might have good advice to offer on how a new club pro could ingratiate himself to the membership. But Lorms could play, too! He managed to play all four rounds at Inverness in the 1920 Open. Lorms had just been installed as the professional at Columbus Country Club—a position he would hold for thirty-seven years. During his tenure there, he found time to design two notable courses in the Columbus environs: Brookside and Worthington Hills. With its strategic doglegs and elevated greens, Brookside has the look of a Donald Ross course. Lorms's familiarity with Inverness and Columbus (both Donald Ross designs) undoubtedly influenced his work.

Although he was off line with some of his long tee shots, Gullickson was the star of the match on the front nine, leading his team to a three-up lead. Despite his team's deficit, George Sargent was the most consistent player, "his drives being in the fairway most of the time, and his putts always going for the cup." However, unfamiliarity with yardages (there were no yardage markers back then) cost Sargent a better score. Charlie kept the Lorms-Gullickson partnership comfortably ahead on the back nine with some inspired play of his own, and the two younger men prevailed 4 and 3. Elks members had to be pleased that their new pro had made a good showing by defeating a former U.S. Open champion.

Best of all was the fact that the course received rave reviews from the scribes. The *Dispatch*'s Karl Finn wrote that the "natural beauty of the course attracted the spectators and golfers as much as the play did." Moreover, the "many trees and the stream that runs through the course add to its splendid appearance." Finn was particularly partial to the 137-yard, par-three fourteenth over a small lake, which he rated "the most interesting hole." He also liked the first hole, "an attractive dog's leg to the left which will require a long straight drive to clear the ditch and stay on the fairway." The *Ohio State Journal*'s Peniston penned that The Elks "is a beautiful spot, different from other local courses except Winding Hollow [now Champions] which is somewhat similar. It affords restful views to the eyes and cooling shade along the way where one may stop and enjoy it all when not bent on a record-breaking score. It is a course that will grow on one and never grow dull or tiresome, and be a spot perhaps like many of the English courses—one that golfers will like to go back once in a while and enjoy it—especially the first nine holes."

John W. and Harold Kaufman had to be thrilled with the positive press. But even in the glow of the course's smash opening, the Elks could not rest. There

GOLF IN COLUMBUS AT WYANDOT COUNTRY CLUB

The mainstays of The Elks Country Club staff in 1924, including greenkeeper Lawrence Huber and golf professional Lloyd Gullickson (second and third from left, respectively). *From the* Ohio State Journal, *May 11, 1924.*

was the need to obtain new Elks—particularly golfing Elks—to defray expenses of operation. The course was thus opened to the public the following Monday, Tuesday, Thursday and Friday in hopes of gaining a few more members.

Lloyd Gullickson worked as The Elks' professional through the 1926 golf season. In this madcap era of flagpole sitting and marathon dancing, "Gully" took part in a similar act of tomfoolery. Perched precariously atop Columbus's new forty-seven-story downtown AIU tower (now the LeVeque Tower), he drove a golf ball far into the distance. Afterward, he moved to Westwood Country Club in Cleveland for the 1927 season. He won the Ohio Open in 1934 and later became the professional at Inverness in 1945. Gullickson had a tough act to follow at Inverness, as he succeeded Byron Nelson as the club's professional. He served there until he retired in 1965. But one of his most interesting golf experiences was the match he played in 1934, partnering with the incomparable Babe Didrikson against Glenna Collett Vare (at the time the best female player) and her partner, Babe Ruth. Didrikson was just learning the game, having won Olympic medals in track and field just two years before. But she was much further along in becoming proficient at the game than baseball's Babe, and she and Gullickson won easily.

The year 1923 also saw another significant development adjacent to The Elks. In order to speed up its interurban operations, the Columbus, Delaware & Marion Railway Company opened the Worthington Bypass, a portion of which was routed along the eastern border of the property. Players were treated to the sight of the interurban scooting by the premises until 1933.

Chapter 5

EXPLORING THE LOST COURSE

Let's take a time capsule back to the heyday of The Elks/Wyandot and have a look at the course. A good place to start is with the scorecard. The yardage of 6,393 was fairly typical for courses in an era when the best drives of top professionals were 240 to 250 yards. The par fours were particularly challenging. The scorecard shows six par fours over 400 yards. The par fives (there were only three of them on this par-seventy-one layout) were on the short side. It appears that separate ladies' tees were not built, and their markers on most holes were probably located a few yards ahead of the regular tees. This might account for the high women's par of seventy-eight strokes.

One of Ross's design principles was to avoid having two successive holes routed in the same direction. The course map demonstrates that this was achieved at The Elks/Wyandot. Ross did not like to see a player top his ball and have it run like a rabbit over the largely un-watered fairways of the time onto the green. Thus, he often placed skull-eating cross bunkers on these holes well short of the green to keep the player from being rewarded for a bad shot. Such cross bunkers can be discerned on holes seven and seventeen. The driveway (still in the same location now) accesses the property from Morse Road and then heads generally north before gradually winding its way easterly over to the clubhouse. The tenth hole (originally number one on The Elks) is routed at nearly a right angle. Brookside member Dwight Watkins, who caddied and played at Wyandot as a boy, remembers this severe dogleg hole fondly.

GOLF IN COLUMBUS AT WYANDOT COUNTRY CLUB

Above: Another Elks hole featuring an uphill shot to a well-bunkered green. *Betty Huber collection.*

Left: This 1936 Wyandot scorecard shows a round played by Wyandot star Johnny Florio. *Judith Florio collection.*

Opposite, top: This diagram of the course dating from the 1948 Columbus Invitational was published after the nines were reversed sometime subsequent to 1936. *Courtesy of Gary Parsons.*

Opposite, bottom: The county auditor's map of the 265 acres purchased by the BPOE in 1921. *Courtesy of Franklin County auditor.*

The Elks Years, 1922-31

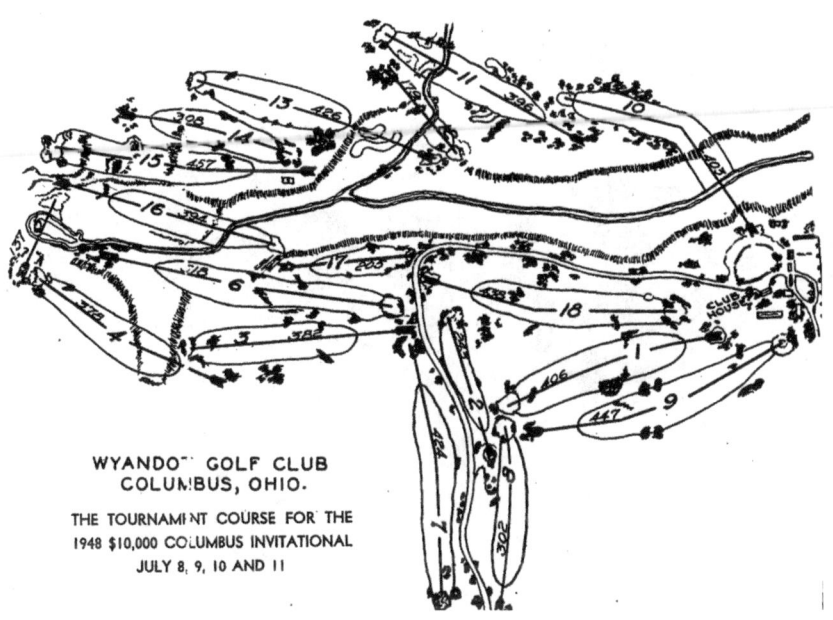

WYANDOT GOLF CLUB
COLUMBUS, OHIO.

THE TOURNAMENT COURSE FOR THE
1948 $10,000 COLUMBUS INVITATIONAL
JULY 8, 9, 10 AND 11

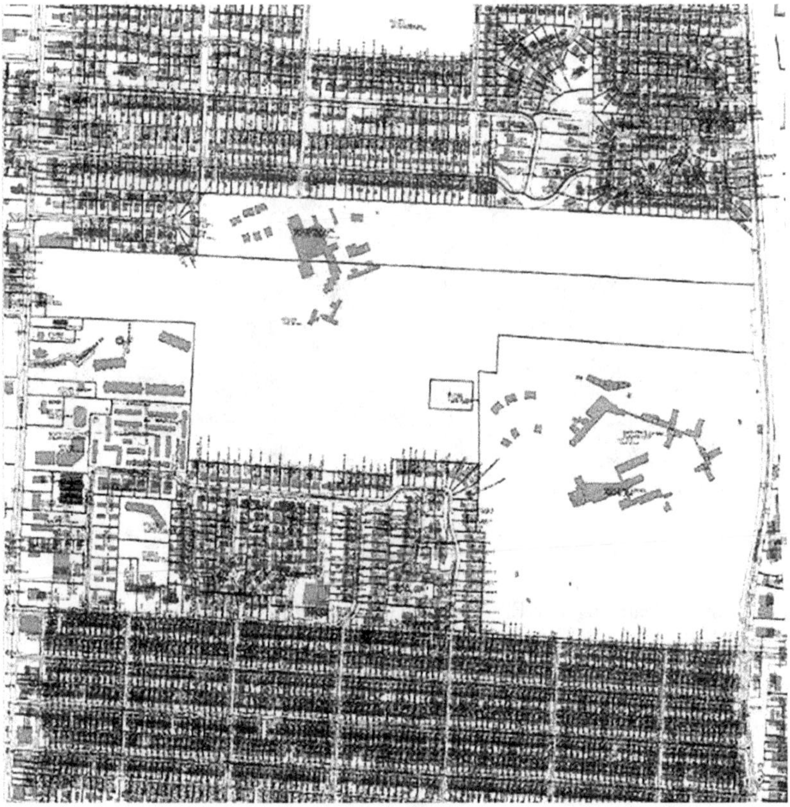

Skylarks' cartoon featuring The Elks Country Club. *From the* Columbus Sunday Dispatch, *June 26, 1927.*

Opposite: Membership bill from The Elks. *Mike Hurdzan collection.*

The Elks Years, 1922-31

The current county auditor's map shows in white the entire 265 acres that John W. Kaufman bought for the BPOE in 1921. The footprint of the property looks something akin to a snub-nosed gun. The buildings depicted on the lower right of the map are those on the campus of the School for the Deaf. The buildings shown on the upper left of the auditor's map house the School for the Blind. The driveway to the latter school is accessed from High Street and comes down the short "barrel" of the gun.

The Elks' members no doubt chuckled when they opened the June 26, 1927 *Sunday Dispatch* and found cartoonist Dudley T. Fisher Jr.'s full-page "Skylarks" cartoon featuring The Elks Country Club, which poked some gentle fun at the membership. The cartoon is replete with "inside" humor, although a couple of the asides can be understood. One figure is identified as star player Denny Shute, who is "looking over his mail." Shute was having a sensational 1927 golf season and receiving plenty of press. Lawrence Huber (center of the drawing) is said to be "keeping his eye on the works," as a greenkeeper would be doing. The Locker Room Quartet's singing was a known hallmark of the club's social life. Fisher's depiction is invaluable in showing detail of the club's infrastructure, course and surroundings. The clubhouse, turreted outbuilding, driveway and holes one, seven, nine, ten, sixteen, seventeen and eighteen (Wyandot holes ten, sixteen, eighteen, one, seven, eight and nine, respectively) are detailed. So are the adjacent farming operations, the adjacent WAIV radio tower and the CD&M interurban.

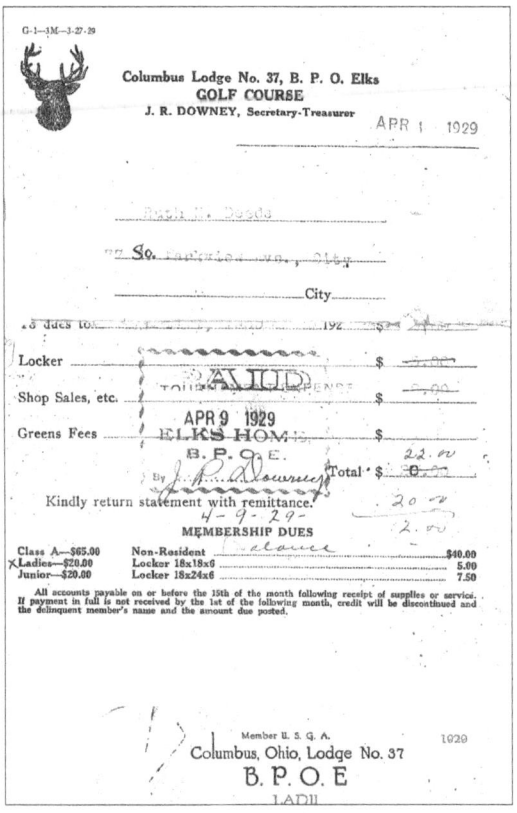

Chapter 6
DENNY SHUTE AND THE "MAKER OF CHAMPIONS"

Lloyd Gullickson's resignation after the 1926 season necessitated the search for a new golf professional. The opening attracted two hundred applications. On January 20 1927, The Elks Country Club announced the hiring of Hermon Shute, most recently the pro at Spring Valley Country Club in Huntington, West Virginia. Like Scioto's pro, George Sargent, forty-nine-year-old Shute had come to America from England in 1901. Like many of the old pros who emigrated from the old sod, Hermon was an accomplished club maker. It was also noted in the announcement that Hermon's twenty-two-year-old son, Densmore, "has twice been amateur champion of West Virginia." However, it would have been natural for local golf pundits to question whether triumphs in the less golf-developed Mountain State would translate to success for Denny in hotly competitive Columbus. Would he even win The Elks' club championship?

Quiet, reserved Denny made an immediate splash by setting the amateur course record at The Elks. All who watched him were impressed with his Fred Couples–like "swing easy, hit hard" style. He raised eyebrows further in mid-June by qualifying along with pros Charlie Lorms and George Sargent for the upcoming U.S. Open. He was just getting started. The week following the Open qualifier found Denny competing at Walnut Cliffs (another name for Columbus Country Club) in the local district amateur championship tournament. With only one close call, Shute cruised through his matches to the thirty-six-hole final. Perhaps emulating movie star Ronald Colman, Denny sported a trim mustache when facing Scioto's E. Cutler

The Elks Years, 1922-31

Dawes. Shute won easily, 8 and 7. However, his victory took a backseat to another headliner, Charles Lindbergh, who was being fêted in New York upon his return from France.

After receiving the "Dispatch Trophy" for his District Amateur win, Denny motored east to Wheeling, where he spent the night en route to the U.S. Open, which was to start on Thursday at Pittsburgh's Oakmont. Oakmont, then as now, was an extraordinarily difficult test. The "Silver Scot" Tommy Armour wound up the winner with an inflated tally of 301! Denny did not break 80, but the course was so brutal that his 325 total still brought him a T-48 finish in his first foray on a national stage. He finished fifth low amateur (low am was always the property of Bobby Jones). Low Columbus player honors went to forty-five-year-old George Sargent, who outdid Denny by three shots.

Denny Shute after receiving the Dispatch Trophy for winning the Columbus District Championship. *From the* Columbus Sunday Dispatch, *June 12, 1927.*

After his Saturday finish in Pittsburgh, Denny raced to Dayton to compete in the Ohio Amateur at Miami Valley Country Club. It would have been understandable had he sagged some after this whirlwind of pressure-filled competitive golf. But Denny stayed focused, and his run of great golf continued with a win over Sinclair Dean in the event's final match. Shute's victory marked the first statewide championship won by a Columbus-based player. It would not be the last. Other Elks players would validate Denny's triumph with their own victories in the state amateur. There was a harbinger of this coming success in the Elks team's victory at the 1927 district team championship. The Elks team of Denny, Bill Deuschle, Bob Albright and F.C. Eickmeyer stormed to the title at Walnut Cliffs by nine shots over Scioto!

Having dominated the amateurs, Shute entered the professional ranks at the beginning of the 1928 season to gauge his capability of competing with

Golf in Columbus at Wyandot Country Club

the likes of Tommy Armour, Walter Hagen and Gene Sarazen. But his great golf at The Elks was not over. In August 1928, Denny fired what the press deemed a "miracle" round of 62 over his old home course. Shute's course record would never be equaled.

With Denny Shute gone from the scene of Ohio amateur golf, another Elks stalwart stepped up in 1928. Bill Deuschle was well regarded in local golf circles. He had come close to carrying off district honors several times while an Elks member. Bill switched his membership over to Arlington Golf Club just prior to entering the '28 district championship at Scioto. Things went well for Bill at Scioto, as he vanquished every opponent en route to the final. His victims included Alfred Sargent (George's son) and talented high schooler Johnny Florio. Furthermore, his wife, Martha, likewise made it to the final of the Ladies' Franklin County Amateur. Bill's game went dreadfully awry in the last match against Raleigh W. Lee, who was advantaged by competing on his home course. After a woeful 84 in the morning round of the final, Deuschle found himself buried 5 down to Lee. He played better in the afternoon but was still soundly trounced 5 and 3. Martha, however, salvaged some family pride by coming home a winner in her event.

Frustrated by another near miss, Bill resolved to give it another go in the '28 Ohio Amateur at Youngstown Country Club (yet another Ross design). He again played beautifully all the way to the final, where he was matched against four-time state amateur champion Harold Weber of Toledo. This time, it was Deuschle who emerged from the morning with a five-up lead. It appeared that Bill might let another title slip away when Weber cut the lead to two after twenty-three holes. But that rally sputtered, and Deuschle won a close, albeit spottily played, final 2 and 1. While the James M. Cox Trophy technically traveled down the road to Arlington, a piece of it surely belonged at The Elks. The club members took great pride in the knowledge that a second Elks-honed player had become the state amateur champion.

An Elks junior member claimed the club's third-straight Ohio Amateur in 1929 at Canton Brookside. However, this victory could not be categorized as a total surprise. Great things had been predicted for Johnny Florio since 1926, when, still a schoolboy, he claimed the Columbus district amateur title. He followed up that success with four municipal championships and a semifinal appearance in the U.S. Publinx tournament in '28 prior to joining The Elks. Johnny, one of fifteen children, was blessed with natural athletic ability and starred in football, basketball and baseball at Columbus's West High. But golf was his first love, and he immersed himself in the game, playing and caddying every chance he could. He became such a sought-

The Elks Years, 1922-31

after "looper" that he toted for the likes of Bobby Jones, Walter Hagen and Gene Sarazen in prestigious events like the U.S. Open, U.S. Amateur and PGA. Johnny closely observed these great players. It was said that his swing was a carbon copy of Sarazen's, who, like Johnny, was born of Italian immigrants. By the time he joined The Elks in '29, young Johnny was already a seasoned campaigner with plenty of tournament experience. Florio confidently breezed through the field at Canton Brookside. Sparked by a holed bunker shot, he defeated Cincinnati's Neil Remsick in the final match, 4 and 3. Golf writers across the state took note of the fact that Florio's victory was the third consecutive win in the Ohio Amateur by three different Elks golfers!

Johnny Florio, 1929 and 1932 Ohio Amateur champion. *From the* Columbus Evening Dispatch, *July 17, 1932.*

When the 1930 Ohio Amateur at Toledo Country Club rolled around, Johnny Florio led a contingent of six golfers from The Elks northward. Johnny was favored to make it four consecutive Elks winners. But Florio, hampered by an infection in his left forearm, was dispatched in the third round. It appeared that that the Elks' streak surely would end. However, one of the lesser known of the club's better players kept hopes alive by somehow golfing his ball into the semis. Glen Bishop, a twenty-six-year-old clerk for the Ohio Auto Club who was making his first appearance in a noteworthy event, was fortunate to qualify for match play. Glen himself wondered whether he was being foolhardy to journey to Toledo for the event. He felt he had no chance to win, and he could "hardly spare the time or money necessary to make the trip." But Bishop, playing brilliantly, manufactured one upset after another. His victories included the previous year's runner-up, Neil Remsick, as well as Nelson Ruddy, the 1929 medalist. The press suddenly realized that Bishop was

Glen Bishop, 1930 Ohio Amateur champion. *From the* Columbus Citizen, *June 27, 1930*.

playing as well as anyone, having recorded solid rounds of 75-72-73 in his victories. In the semis, he faced Raleigh Lee, the 1928 Columbus district champion and many-time contender for state honors. Surely Glen's joyride would end. But instead he stayed hot, garnering another surprise victory, 3 and 2.

Amazingly, Glen Bishop had played his way into the final. His opponent would be young Toledo insurance salesman Ray Miller, who would have the advantage of hometown support. The combination of a showdown featuring a complete unknown against a local hero drew one thousand spectators to the final. Glen started slowly and found himself 3 down after thirteen. But by winning three of the last five holes of the morning round, he squared the match heading to lunch.

The afternoon eighteen was closely contested all the way. With the match dead even at the long par-three fourteenth, Miller came up just short of the green, leaving a straightforward chip. Bishop put himself in serious trouble after an atrociously hooked mid-iron. His ball came to rest forty yards from the hole in a road rut on "hard clay with a downhill lie and a knob just beside it," according to *Dispatch* reporter Lathop Mack. Glen asked the referee whether his ball was in a hazard. He was told it was not but that he nevertheless would not be permitted to ground his club on the hardpan. In Mack's view, this was "a trifle ambiguous ruling." Facing what appeared to be certain loss of the hole, and the match's turning point, Bishop executed

The Elks Years, 1922-31

a pitch that would be remembered for years to come. Laying back the face of his niblick, Glen "scooped the ball well up and dropped on the green. It trickled up to within inches of the hole." Stunned by this improbable recovery and the accompanying reversal of fortunes, Miller came up short with his own chip and then missed the tying putt. Bishop was ahead for the first time! He nursed his one-up lead to the eighteenth green, where he stood shaking over a twelve-incher for bogey 5 to close out the tournament. Upon holing it, Glen "dropped his club and turned around wearily to grasp Miller's outstretched hand." In a gesture of fine sportsmanship, Miller invited Bishop to play Ray's home club of Inverness the following day. The most unlikely of The Elks' fine players had been the one to stretch the club's victory string to four. Just to illustrate the depth of fine players at The Elks, none of the club's vaunted Ohio Amateur champions made it to the finals of the club championship that year. Joe Outhwaite bested Stark Frambes in the thirty-six-hole final.

The Elks' Ohio Amateur victory string finally came to an end in 1931. But a second Johnny Florio victory in 1932 at Portage Country Club in Akron made it five out of six wins. As Lathop Mack put it, the James M. Cox Trophy "was on its way back to its old shelf, to be gloated over by the members there for another year." The Elks' greens committee chairman, Tom Dempsey, told the *Citizen*'s Lew Byrer why Elks players enjoyed such tremendous tournament success: "The reason is simple enough. Our course is so designed that you have to shoot accurate golf to score well. It's accurate golf which wins. Players used to our course, lined on both sides by trees, ravines, and other troubles, find it comparatively easy to score on the more open courses over which most tournaments are played." Byrer's column further noted that "holes 1, 2, 4, 5, 6, 7, 8, 9, 11, 12, 13, 14, 15, 16, and 17 are lined on one or both sides by trees or out-of-bounds hazards designed to catch the wildly sliced or hooked tee shot...To score well over the Elks' course, you've got to stay down the middle or thereabouts all the time."

Meanwhile, Denny Shute's pro career was cresting. While failing to post a win in his 1928 campaign, Denny demonstrated a hint of things to come with a stellar T-6 at the U.S. Open. In '29, he broke through with his first win in the Ohio Open. Denny really hit his stride in 1930, recording three wins at the Texas and Los Angeles Opens and a repeat triumph in the Ohio Open. Perhaps Denny had an unfair advantage in the latter triumph, as it was staged at The Elks! But the course held up very well to the onslaughts of Denny and his fellow pros. His winning score in windy weather was 287—an average of almost 72 per round. Anxious to capitalize on the

GOLF IN COLUMBUS AT WYANDOT COUNTRY CLUB

Denny Shute (second from left) accepts the Wanamaker Trophy for winning the 1937 PGA Championship at Pittsburgh Field Club. *From the* Ohio State Journal, *May 31, 1937.*

success of its hometown boy, the *Columbus Citizen* picked Denny to author a golf tip column, "Shooting with Shute."

A runner-up finish in the 1931 PGA Championship (played at match play until 1958) was just the first of his great performances in that tournament. From 1933 to 1937, Denny Shute was arguably the best player in the world. No player matched Denny's three major championships victories during that span. In 1933, he took home the Open Championship at the "Home of Golf," St. Andrews, on his first trip across the pond, besting fellow American Craig Wood in a thirty-six-hole playoff. In '36, he displayed his growing dominance at match play by winning the PGA Championship at Ross's beloved Pinehurst No. 2, where he defeated the tour's longest driver, Jimmy Thompson, 3 and 2 in the final.

In the following year's PGA championship at Pittsburgh Field Club, Shute rallied from a 2-down deficit with four holes to play to catch Jug McSpaden. He won the match on the thirty-seventh hole. Denny was the last player to win two consecutive PGAs until Tiger Woods accomplished the feat more than sixty years later. His match play success was no accident. The three-time Ryder

The Elks Years, 1922-31

Cupper's combination of down-the-middle shotmaking with an unruffled demeanor unnerved many an opponent. In all, Shute won seventeen PGA tour events. His résumé includes seven top-tens in the U.S. Open. His high-water mark in that event occurred in the 1941 championship at sweltering Colonial in Fort Worth, where he finished runner-up to Craig Wood, who thereby gained a bit of revenge for his finals loss to Denny in the '37 PGA.

Like his fellow competitors of the era, Denny kept a club affiliation to supplement the scanty purses available on tour. Upon turning professional, he was hired by York Temple—only a couple miles north of The Elks. In 1930, Shute moved over to Brookside Golf and Country Club to join his father, Hermon, who had taken the club pro job there after his short stint at The Elks. Denny served as the club's "touring pro," while Hermon manned the pro shop and gave most of the lessons. Thereafter, Denny became something of a nomad, serving at a number of different clubs in different states (including Lake Forest Country Club in my hometown of Hudson, Ohio) until landing for good at Portage Country Club in Akron in 1945.

Denny Shute did not have occasion to golf much in Columbus until two tournaments in 1950. He entered the PGA at Scioto, hosting its first major championship since the 1926 U.S. Open. Now forty-five, and well past his prime, Shute had not been a factor in the event since the '30s. But he qualified for match play, won two matches and made the round of sixteen before bowing to Jimmy Demaret. Encouraged by his improved form, he signed up for a second Columbus event later in the summer—the Ohio Open at rain-soaked Brookside, a club Denny had served as pro eighteen years before. Brandishing a hot putter, Denny was in the thick of things with a score of 140 through the first two rounds.

Thursday's concluding double round was mostly played in a downpour. While conditions were not ideal, they failed to deter Denny, who was experiencing the ultimate in "sentimental journeys." Accompanied in the drenching rain by his wife, Hettie (a Columbus girl whom he married at St. John's Episcopal Church in Worthington in 1930), and daughter Nancy, Denny blitzed Brookside with a 67-69 finish. His sweet fifty-yard pitch-in for eagle on hole eleven of the morning round kick-started his blazing stretch run culminating in his fourth Ohio Open title. It was fitting that Shute's last big win took place in the same locale where he had launched his playing career. Unfortunately, the course at which his career really took off, The Elks, was on life support by then.

Years later, as *Dispatch* sportswriter Russ Needham was bemoaning the apparent imminent closing of Wyandot, he recalled that "there was a time when Wyandot was called the 'maker of champions,' and there may have been something to the story. Its tree-lined fairways did demand straight shooting, and its small greens prescribed accuracy. Whatever it had, it produced champions year after year in the late 1920's. There was Denny Shute, Bill Deuschle, Johnny Florio, Glen Bishop and Mel Carpenter among the men, and of the women there was the late Mrs. Thornton Emmons, Mrs. Martha Deuschle, and more recently, Sally Elson, all of them champions."

Unfortunately, two of The Elks' and Wyandot's Ohio Amateur champions, like the course that helped "make" them, met premature demises. Glen Bishop passed away in 1953 at the age of fifty-three. His obituary noted that he had fought back from crippling arthritis that had left him bedridden for two years but "had been playing in the '70's again at Brookside [which he joined after Wyandot closed] last summer." Dwight Watkins, a Brookside member since 1948, remembers playing rounds with Glen Bishop. Dwight still uses a tip Glen imparted to him: "He told me, 'Dwight, always see the clubface hit the ball.'"

Johnny Florio died of a heart attack in 1966 at age fifty-eight. Winner of two district and state amateurs by age twenty-four, Johnny ranks second only to Denny Shute in the pantheon of The Elks/Wyandot's array of great players. This all-around athlete certainly possessed the talent to turn professional. Instead, he worked as an account executive for a Chicago athletic equipment firm while continuing to compete in state and local amateur events.

Denny Shute continued as the professional at Portage in Akron until his retirement in 1972. Although his tournament appearances were infrequent, he continued to work on his game and carded a 66 to match his age in 1971. One of the Portage members joked, "The only time you could get Denny to give you a lesson was if you were his partner and you were two down." Shute died in Akron in 1974 at the age of sixty-nine. He was elected to the World Golf Hall of Fame in 2008. Sam Snead paid tribute to Shute, acknowledging that "if he had the fever to play tournament golf, he'd have been the equal to me."

Denny Shute and his fellow Elks stalwarts dominated the Ohio amateur golf scene in the 1927–32 time period in a fashion that was never duplicated by the members of any other club before or since. The "Roaring Twenties" is often referred to as sports' "Golden Age." That designation certainly applied to the golf played at The Elks Country Club—the "Maker of Champions" in this halcyon period.

Chapter 7
THE INVENTOR

Many remarkable characters played their roles on The Elks/Wyandot stage during its too-brief existence. The Kaufmans, Denny Shute, Johnny Florio and others we have yet to encounter are all luminaries who contributed to the club and course. But of all the illustrious personages encountered in researching the club's history, I admire most the club's longtime greenkeeper, Lawrence Huber. I admit to bias on this point, as in the course of this project, I became friendly with Lawrence Huber's son Jim, his daughter-in-law Betty and his grandson Bill. But I suspect objective observers would concur that Lawrence Huber deserves the praise I heap on him in this account.

He certainly overcame a tough start in life. Born in 1893, he was orphaned at age two and spent most of the next fourteen years being cared for at the "Odd Fellows' Home for Orphans, Indigent, and the Aged" located in Springfield—about an hour west of Columbus. The Independent Order of Odd Fellows was founded in England and brought to America in 1819. The order dedicated itself to the proposition that "the strong support the weak, the well nurse the sick, the learned instruct the unlearned, and the rich help the poor." The Springfield home, opened in 1898, was largely self-sufficient with its own farming operation, which provided the home with fresh produce, dairy products and meat.

For many, the image of a turn-of-the-century orphanage conjures up a bleak specter of a desultory poorhouse where unfortunate children lived a life of hardship, experiencing little in the way of love, comfort, education

Golf in Columbus at Wyandot Country Club

Lawrence Huber. *Betty Huber collection.*

or useful training. Indeed, the number of orphanages dwindled during the 1900s as foster care and other care arrangements surpassed them in public favor. Lawrence Huber left the Odd Fellows' Home in 1909 at age sixteen with the equivalent of an eighth-grade education. But whether it was in spite of or because of his residence there, he nevertheless emerged with an impressive skill set. He possessed high aptitude for working with motors and other mechanical devices; he had no trouble taking them apart and putting them back together again. While his reading and writing abilities were not exemplary at this stage of his life, he offset this limitation with an uncanny ability to perform complicated arithmetic problems in his head. He was also a young man who did not shy away from hard labor. Lawrence was well aware that it would take unstinting work on his part to overcome his underprivileged beginnings.

The orphanage arranged for Lawrence's first outside employment at a farm in Jackson County, Ohio, in the foothills of Appalachia, about an hour south of Columbus. The mechanical implements available to farmers were extremely rudimentary, and farmers were often faced with the task of having to repair these implements on their own without instruction manuals

The Elks Years, 1922-31

to help. It is likely that the need for trial-and-error problem solving at the farm resulted in exceptional training for his job at The Elks/Wyandot.

Always looking to better himself, Lawrence moved from the farm and took a position in Columbus with the Pennsylvania Railroad. He was employed there as an "express messenger." Typically, Huber would ride the rails between Columbus and St. Louis (a route over the portion of the Pennsy's lines called the "Panhandle") and be gone from home for days at a time. During his railroad days, Lawrence met Eunice Daugherty, who lived on a farm in Alton, a tiny hamlet just west of Columbus on the National Road. It seemed a good match, for sure, but Lawrence was probably a little hesitant to get hitched because his required absences from Columbus would likely not be conducive to matrimonial bliss.

Fate intervened when Lawrence got wind of the greenkeeper opening at The Elks Country Club in the spring of 1922. At first blush, it is surprising he was considered for the position since it is doubtful he had ever stepped foot on a golf course. But he had a couple things going for him. There were still farming operations at the property, a holdover activity from the Higgins estate days. Lawrence had that base covered. Secondly, he was a young man of twenty-eight who could grow with the club. Also, The Elks' management presumably concluded that Lawrence had shown evidence of being a quick study who could learn on the job by observing Donald Ross, soon to be at work laying out the course.

Lawrence would have eventually married Eunice even if The Elks' management had not told him in no uncertain terms that the club wanted a married man to fill the post. But his desire to obtain the job certainly hurried the nuptials along. In short order, Mr. and Mrs. Lawrence Huber occupied the frame house on the property that the club had reserved for the greenkeeper. Eunice was very supportive of Lawrence's career, accompanying him to various state and national greenkeeper association conclaves. Eunice bore Lawrence three children: Bill, Jane and Jim. By all accounts, the Hubers were a happy family. Lawrence and Eunice made good friends with their fellow greenkeepers, such as Bridgeview's Grube and Columbus Country Club's Hoover families. Marilyn Gohlke Strasser (mother of Dan Strasser, a several-time Brookside Golf and Country Club champion) remembers wonderful picnics shared by the Gohlke and Huber families. Many were held at the Huber residence adjacent to the golf course. Marilyn's mother, Lydia, met Eunice when they worked together at Smith Hardware in downtown Columbus. And seventy-five years have not dimmed Marilyn's fond memories of Lawrence. "He was a great man whom you looked up

Lawrence Huber and his wife, Eunice. *Betty Huber collection.*

to," she said. "He was kind to all of us kids. He was a quiet but strong man. And he would play the accordion at our get-togethers quite well! The Hubers were a very musical family. They were a close-knit family who helped each other out. My understanding is that there were even a few occasions where Eunice helped out with the mowing of the greens when Lawrence was short-staffed."

Lawrence Huber had a unique opportunity to learn from the best. He accompanied Donald Ross when the great architect staked The Elks in 1922.

The Elks Years, 1922-31

Since he was brand new to the game at that time, Lawrence probably had no concept of Ross's importance in the world of golf. Still, he was amazed how the architect, with nothing more than a level in his hand, could quickly and unerringly determine appropriate tiling to enhance drainage. Ross believed attention to drainage to be the single most important factor in golf course design and maintenance, and Huber took the lessons imparted by Ross on this subject to heart. Lawrence also immersed himself in the details of The Elks' manual fairway sprinkling system—a high-end investment for the fledgling club.

In 1922, greenkeeping was still a relatively new profession. Production of maintenance equipment was in its infancy. The best turf for golf and methods for avoiding weeds, topdressing and rolling of greens, as well as myriad other aspects of maintenance, were subjects still open for debate. To figure out for himself the solutions to the problems of his trade, Lawrence voraciously read the greenkeepers' trade journal, *The National Greenkeeper*, and became actively involved in the National Association of Greenkeepers of America when it was formed in 1926. Though his formal scientific training at the orphanage was minimal, he habitually applied the scientific method in testing the efficacy of material applications.

Renowned golf course architect Bill Amick, who grew up near the course and knew the Huber family well, recalls one such experiment by Lawrence. It involved the circular and slightly hogback-shaped first green. Amick relates:

> *It was not only a green but also a test plot for seven or eight varieties of bent grasses. Those were planted like pieces cut out of a pie. Lawrence wanted to study and compare how various bents performed under actual course conditions. He told me that one problem with this test was that changing cup locations took extra effort in order to avoid the introduction of one kind of grass into another piece of the pie. This would have happened using the conventional method of simply placing a plug of sod from the new cup into the old cup in a section of different bent grass.*

Lawrence became so enthused over his various tests that he eventually began writing about them in *The National Greenkeeper*. An example of this was his published letter discussing how he dealt with an outbreak of small brown patch. He prepared an experimental plot of ten strips, each ten feet wide, and then applied ten different fertilizers on each individual strip. He found the best fertilizer for small brown patch to be "cotton seed meal, 100 pounds per 5000 square feet." Lawrence added, "For large brown patch, I top dress greens with good compost and apply sulphate of ammonia, the rate dependent on how hot the weather is." He also reported to the magazine's readers that lighter rollers worked better on its bent-grass greens (son Jim says that his father told him that at the time it was planted, The Elks was the only eighteen-hole course in the United States where all the greens were planted in "creeping bent" grass). Lawrence's findings were based on a test over several weeks in which lighter rollers were applied to the greens of The Elks' front nine while simultaneously using heavier rollers on the back-side greens.

Huber even weighed in on the subject of whether greenkeepers should play golf. Though he had trouble breaking 100, he expressed the view that it was a good idea to play occasionally because the greenkeeper could thereby "find out the condition of the course in the way that regular members have of finding out." Lawrence recommended playing with the pro or green committee members early in the morning, as this affords the greenkeeper an opportunity to "bring up anything pertaining to the improvement of the course."

Lawrence's ability to conceive of and fabricate workable maintenance machinery was astonishing. He found a way to use a gasoline-powered motor to agitate pressure-filled tanks to apply fungicide to the greens. When weed killer came into use around 1944, he used a similar apparatus at Brookside to spray the fairways. This eliminated the omnipresent white milky dandelions (often confused at a distance with golf balls) that had previously plagued course maintenance. Lawrence's best and most complex innovation was his motorized "spiker," used to aerate the fairways and greens.

Lawrence Huber's experiments with technology were not limited to golf course maintenance equipment. In 1927, he assembled the forerunner of a television. His short-wave receiver was able to pick up a discernible silhouette image sent by a signal from Washington, D.C.

Lawrence's insatiable thirst for knowledge led him to enroll in agronomy courses at Purdue University. His professional achievements led his peers to name him president of the Ohio Golf Superintendents Association in 1939 (Lawrence succeeded in his campaign to change the job title to "superintendent," which he felt better described the job's comprehensive administrative duties). The poor orphan with an eighth-grade education had definitely pulled himself up by his bootstraps! Lawrence was proud that he had come so far and thus was never reluctant to reveal his humble background.

Lawrence Huber served as greenkeeper (or superintendent, as he would prefer) for The Elks/Wyandot from 1922 to 1943. He then left the club and signed up as an agronomist with the U.S. Corps of Army Engineers. The family was afforded government housing in Columbus, but Lawrence

The Elks Years, 1922-31

Right: Pressure-filled tanks applying fungicide at The Elks. *Betty Huber collection.*

Below: Lawrence Huber's spiker. *Betty Huber collection.*

traveled to air bases in five states to work on landscaping projects. According to son Jim, there were two reasons Lawrence left Wyandot and joined the corps: (1) he was disappointed that the government had exempted him from service during World War I because it did not want to take farmers into the service, and he thought that joining the corps during the new conflict would be of service to his country; and (2) he could see the "handwriting on the wall" noting that Wyandot's days as a private club were numbered. In Lawrence's view, a private club's members always helped the greenkeeper care for the course by repairing ball marks and divots. That was not generally the case with public golf courses. Lawrence probably would have acknowledged that he was a little spoiled on this point, but he simply had no interest in dealing with the headaches that go with maintaining a public facility.

In the course of his service with the corps of engineers, Lawrence directed labor performed by German prisoners of war. The officer in charge of the prisoners refused to allow them sufficient water breaks even during broiling summer weather. Huber registered complaints up the chain of command and sought humane treatment for the prisoners but was rebuffed. Disenchanted with the officers' conduct, Lawrence sought and obtained an early exit from the corps in 1944.

Lawrence soon was back in the course superintendent business, this time with Brookside Golf and Country Club in Columbus. Brookside's course had suffered terribly during the war. The bunkers were solidly laden with weeds, and the membership had dropped to perilously low numbers. Brookside had come close to closing down completely. Son Jim remembers that the family moved into the second floor of the clubhouse above the kitchen. The Hubers had never paid for housing since Lawrence and Eunice had been married, but the cramped living conditions convinced the couple that it was time to own their home. After six months in the clubhouse, the Hubers found one to their liking and moved into their own residence.

Brookside was in such a precarious financial position at that time that Lawrence had to accomplish most of the work without staff. Jim recalls that the greens committee chairman, Harvey Bible, offered him a job when he was just twelve. Jim wound up clearing weeds at one dollar per bunker. Once Lawrence saw that the weeds were so thick that it was taking the boy a full day to clear a single trap, he pulled him off that project. Under Lawrence Huber's stewardship, Brookside's course was gradually brought back into fine shape. He was gratified that the membership numbers picked up once he turned the condition of the property around.

The Elks Years, 1922–31

After five years at Brookside, Lawrence moved to his last position as superintendent of the two Ohio State University golf courses—the Scarlet and the Gray. Jim continued working with his father in the business until entering the U.S. Air Force. Another worker on Lawrence's OSU crew was the aforementioned course architect Bill Amick. Lawrence facilitated Bill's obtaining a graduate position in turf management at Purdue University, which became the springboard for Amick's still-active career in golf.

While Lawrence was hopeful that his sons would also become superintendents, Jim, having witnessed his father habitually working seven days a week, wanted no part of it. He stayed in New Mexico and went on to a career as an air traffic controller. Son Bill also sought other business opportunities. After marrying Betty, he spent his career with the Columbus Forge and Iron Company. He died eleven years ago. Betty still lives in Columbus, very close to the long-gone golf course that her father-in-law maintained for twenty-one years.

I first learned of Betty Huber when, in the process of a Google search for information about The Elks Country Club, I landed on Shirley Hyatt's excellent Clintonville History blog. Betty was listed as the source for some information and photos of the course contained on the blog. I contacted Shirley to ascertain how to reach Betty. Shirley responded that Betty had recently passed away. Still, I felt it could be productive to contact Betty's surviving family members. I found the obituary for Betty Huber, who had lived on the north side, and called the gentleman listed as her son, Jack Huber. Jack, after hearing me express condolences for his loss and then discuss my golf research project, volunteered that he had just played golf that November day. After five minutes of conversation, he suddenly asked me, "Where was this golf course exactly?" Something was amiss here! While Jack's mother was indeed named Betty Huber, Lawrence Huber was not his grandfather. It dawned on me that there had to be a second Betty Huber in Columbus. Further Internet research paid off, as I found that this Betty—who was the same age as the woman by the same name who had just died—was alive, well and Lawrence Huber's daughter-in-law. Moreover, she possessed a treasure-trove of pictures, scorecards and memories that are sprinkled throughout this story. Betty has been most patient and helpful with this nosy researcher.

Lawrence's daughter Jane was actually the best golfer in the Huber family. She became an accomplished singer, performing with a prominent choral group in Atlanta. Jane died too young of ovarian cancer.

Lawrence Huber passed away from lung cancer in 1958 at age sixty-five while still toiling as Ohio State's superintendent. Jim says no one ever enjoyed his job more than his father. He also says his father was the most honest man he ever knew. When I asked Jim how Lawrence, with his limited education, invented and innovated the way he had, he responded, "I don't know. It's amazing, isn't it?!"

Chapter 8
"INDIAN BILL"—THE LAST OF THE WYANDOTS

Let's go back in time to 1927. Imagine you are a newly initiated member of the Columbus lodge of the BPOE. You decide to take your wife and nine-year-old daughter, Susie, out for the family's first dinner at the "country home" of the Elks—The Elks Country Club. Upon entering the clubhouse's warm and friendly confines, you and your loved ones encounter a wizened yet animated and agile man whose appearance strikes you as definitely incongruous, given the posh environs. Attired in full Native American regalia—complete with headdress, a necklace of eagle claws and beaded moccasins—he seems completely relaxed and at home in the clubhouse's corridor. With the fearlessness reserved only for the young, Susie marches right up to the old man and asks, "Are you a real Indian?"

The old man flashes a warm smile at his young inquisitor and replies, "Why, yes, young lady. I am a full-blooded Wyandot Indian—the last one left of our tribe. You can call me Bill Moose. Others call me 'Indian Bill.' But the name my mother and father gave me when I was born in 1837 is Kihue."

You do the quick math in your head and enter the conversation. "Golly, Mr. Moose, that would make you ninety years of age," you say. "You don't look anywhere near that old!"

"I attribute my long life to living close to nature and observing the custom of my tribe in sleeping outdoors during the summer and one night each month throughout the winter with only one blanket for cover."

Susie asks an appropriate follow-up question: "So do you live in a tepee when you aren't sleeping outside?"

Golf in Columbus at Wyandot Country Club

Bill Moose in full regalia. *Walter Nice collection.*

Bill Moose, ever gentle and patient with children, responds, "I live alone in a small shack right next to the railroad tracks just south of Morse Road and only a few minutes' walk from where we are standing. I cook my food in a single pot, although I sometimes eat my meals here at The Elks."

Your wife, with a note of concern in her voice, asks, "Don't you get lonely living all by yourself out in the woods?"

"No, not at all. Lots of people come visit me at my shack. I tell them stories about the Wyandots and my days with the circus. I guess my place has become something of a tourist attraction. Folks come from all over to

The Elks Years, 1922-31

take my picture and buy postcards or Indian trinkets. And here at The Elks, I have a chance to meet nice people like you. I keep busy walking. You might see me hiking along the railroad track, in the ravine that runs through the course or over by the Scioto River. That river is very meaningful to my people. I was born and spent my early days up the river in what is now Upper Sandusky."

Susie, eyeing the man's elaborate headdress and robes, probes further. "Are you a chief?" she asks.

Moose shakes his head. "No! I received what I am wearing now for the part I played as an Indian rider in the Sells Brothers Circus. I worked with the circus for nine years. I traveled all over the West and Australia, too. Even met Buffalo Bill and Annie Oakley along the way!

"But you asked about chiefs. The greatest was Leatherlips, who was the Wyandot chief during the time my father was alive. He was a man of peace who made friends with the white man after many years of war. Unfortunately, there were other tribes who were angry with Leatherlips for refusing to continue to make war against the settlers. In 1810, a band of those Indians who wanted to fight came to a place about twelve miles north of Columbus along the Scioto River Road [near where the Columbus Zoo is now] and there put Leatherlips to death because of his peaceful intentions. My family and I walked downriver all the way from Upper Sandusky and saw the place where this occurred. We also hunted and fished around here. Our new chief, Pancake, continued to keep the peace with the whites. One reason we stayed peaceful is that our tribe was converted to Christianity by a Methodist missionary."

Susie then asks a question that you were reluctant to ask the old Wyandot: "What happened to the rest of your tribe?"

Bill Moose reflects for a moment, and a look of wistfulness crosses his lined face. "Our tribe was down to about six hundred by 1843," he says. "With all the settlements, there wasn't room for us anymore, and the Wyandots were pushed out of Ohio. Most of our tribe left Upper Sandusky by wagons and buggies for a reservation in Kansas. Twelve families refused to leave, and mine was one of them. I was only six years old at the time. I worked with the settlers doing many different things, including helping them clear their land. The remaining Wyandots either died out or moved away. I am the last one."

"When did you move to Columbus?" you inquire.

"My family first moved down from Upper Sandusky around 1850. After that, my travels took me away to many places, but I always came back to this area. I moved into the shack in 1915 at the age of seventy-eight.

Bill Moose with Mrs. Daugherty (left) holding on to her daughter Eunice Huber (second from left). *Betty Huber collection.*

I had spent time helping settlers clear land nearby here in this place you now call Clintonville, and I felt at home. People have been very good to me here. I intend to stay until 'The Great I Am' calls me."

You and your family are mesmerized and charmed by Bill's storytelling and warmth. But it's time for dinner. As you shake his hand, he invites you up to the shack. "Come on over sometime, and I will tell you about Annie Oakley and Buffalo Bill." He glances at your wife and says, "You and Susie come, too! Women and children are most welcome. Why, just today the greenkeeper's wife, Mrs. Eunice Huber, came with her mother, Mrs. Daugherty."

The old man, still with a remarkable spring in his step, takes his leave. As you enter the dining room, you encounter the club manager. You remark to him, "That Bill Moose is a fascinating man. I take it he is not a member!"

The manager replies, "No, but he is always welcome here at The Elks."

Bill Moose lived until 1937, passing away just two months short of one hundred. It is said that one measure of a man's greatness is how many people attend his funeral. By that measure, Bill Moose was a very great man indeed. The Rutherford Funeral Home reported that Bill's was the largest funeral it ever handled, with an estimated ten thousand to twelve thousand mourners paying their respects. Bill was buried in full ceremonial regalia

The Elks Years, 1922–31

high on a bluff overlooking the Scioto River on Wyandot Hill, located at the intersection of Riverside Drive and Lane Road in what is now Upper Arlington. Worthington's mayor, Leonard Insley, gave the eulogy. Insley, along with others, helped raise funds for a permanent memorial. Today, thirty-nine bowling ball–sized boulders, stacked in the form of a tepee and marked with inscribed drawings of Native Americans, solemnly mark the site of the grave.

I must confess that I lived within a mile of this pocket park for eighteen years yet never visited. Nor did I understand what the tepee of boulders

Bill Moose's grave. *Courtesy of the author.*

high on the bluff signified when I would glance in that direction whizzing by to work downtown. But now on a cold winter day, I trudge through the snow up the hill to the stone tepee. I brush away the snow that covers its base, thereby unveiling the following inscription:

BILL MOOSE

LAST OF THE WYANDOTS BORN 1837, AND WHOSE DEATH IN 1937 MARKS THE PASSING OF THE INDIANS FROM THIS TERRITORY

Further accolades came to Bill Moose posthumously. The ravine bisecting the course that Bill roamed is now known as Bill Moose Ravine, and the little brook running through the ravine is called Bill Moose Run.

What was there about this man, who lived his life virtually penniless and alone in a shack on the railroad right-of-way, that brought forth such an outpouring of tributes and affection? Yes, he was the last of the Wyandots. But there was more to Bill than that. He was one of those rare people whom everyone loved and wanted to know. He told wonderful stories; he enchanted the young and charmed their elders. Kaye Kessler, the dean of Columbus sportswriters, visited Bill's shack often and came to know him well. He recalls that on Sundays, so many people would crowd the railroad track "to get a peek at or close-up [of Bill] as he spun tales" that Kaye and his friends would sometimes be called on to direct traffic. Bill Moose was a teacher, too, preaching love, understanding and the beauty of nature to all within earshot. He demonstrated how to live a rich, full life without material possessions. And he is an important and certainly unique part of the fabric of The Elks/Wyandot that makes its history so special.

Chapter 9
FIRE FORK!

Had The Elks' general manager, John Downey, reclined in his easy chair at his Dawson Avenue home after Sunday dinner on November 2, 1930, and reflected on the club's state of affairs, his thoughts probably would have been dominated by a sense of relief that The Elks had weathered and survived the 1930 season. There was a depression in full swing, and the accompanying financial turmoil had definitely caused an adverse impact on the membership numbers and bottom lines of all golf and country clubs. But Downey could point to a number of successes in 1930. The club had successfully hosted the Ohio Open, recently concluded the first week of October, and an Elks alum, sweet-swinging Denny Shute, had taken first prize. The club's golf team had also won the season-long, district-wide competition. Downey also would have been pleased with professional Francis Marzolf, whom he hired in 1930 to replace Denny's father, Hermon. Francis was turning out to be the consummate club pro—he was personable and well respected by the members, a fine teacher (Mrs. Thornton Emmons credited Marzolf with making her a champion) and no slouch on the course. Francis had qualified for the 1928 U.S. Open and would do so again in 1933. The consensus among the members was that Arlington Country Club's loss (Marzolf's previous post) was The Elks' gain.

Moreover, there was cause for optimism for the coming year, 1931. For the first time, The Elks Country Club had been selected as the site of the Ohio Amateur. This would afford the club an opportunity to showcase its course, which was already being referred to as the "Maker of Champions" by virtue

Golf in Columbus at Wyandot Country Club

of the fact that the last four Ohio Amateur titles had been captured by four different Elks golfers. Some of the best players in town were gravitating to the high level of competition provided by the likes of Johnny Florio, Glen Bishop, Joe Outhwaite and Mel Carpenter. Higher handicappers in Columbus, having observed the course's positive effect on these champions' games, had to be ruminating on whether their games might also benefit from regular outings at The Elks. Downey would have also been highly aware that the movement to repeal prohibition was gathering steam. That obviously was not going to happen overnight, but the prospect of acquiring a liquor license and its accompanying boon to the fortunes of the club had to be comforting.

It is unnecessary to speculate what Ernest Timberlake was up to during the evening of November 2. His activities were well documented by each of Columbus's daily newspapers the following day. As the caretaker of the clubhouse, Timberlake was furnished living quarters on the second floor. Around 8:00 p.m., he descended into the basement for the purpose of tending the coal furnace and banking the fire for the night. He asserted that he "banked the fire the same as I always do." This task accomplished, he climbed upstairs to bed. He later reported the following: "I hadn't got sound to sleep when I was awakened about 9 P.M. The smoke was thick in my room, and I was coughing when I awakened. I think the smoke awakened me." Continuing his account, Ernest reported that he "jumped up and called Lawrence Huber, the greenskeeper, who makes his home in another building nearby," via the club's internal buzzer system.

Thereafter, Timberlake managed to speedily don trousers and shoes and throw a raincoat over his undershirt. He then left his room and attempted to descend the staircase. The smoke was intense, and Timberlake could not see where he was going. He backtracked and decided to exit the building via his bedroom window, after which he was able to access the roof of the clubhouse's front porch. From there, he leaped to safety. The *Columbus Citizen*'s story informed readers that Mr. Timberlake "barely escaped with his life."

Meanwhile, Huber, having heard Timberlake's buzz, immediately telephoned the fire department at 9:12 p.m. Then he sprinted from his home to the clubhouse and, with Timberlake assisting, "emptied a 30-gallon fire extinguisher on the blaze, which [according to Lawrence] was in the basement, near the furnace." Huber ruefully remarked later, "We almost had it out, and another tank would have done the job. We emptied the tank and waited for the firemen to arrive. They made good time, and first used chemical apparatus they carried."

The Elks Years, 1922-31

But the greatest need was water to extinguish the fire. In that respect, first responder Number 13 Engine Company and the four pump and truck companies that followed were confronted with a virtually hopeless scenario. The nearest hydrant, placed at the corner of Morse Road and Indianola Avenue, was located nearly a half mile from the blaze, which was now starting to rage. Number 13 Engine Company did not have enough hose to cover the long distance and was forced to wait for the other companies. Once all responders had arrived with additional equipment, the firefighters were able to lay almost a mile of hose, thus enabling them to finally "throw two streams of water on the blazing building." As if the firemen did not have enough problems, a driving southeast wind was blowing briskly, exponentially fanning the flames. Extinguishment efforts were also complicated by a persistent drizzle that was morphing into sleet.

In short order, the blaze was out of control, and the clubhouse became totally engulfed in flames. Reluctantly, the firemen abandoned hope of saving the clubhouse and "turned their efforts to watching surrounding trees and leaves to see they did not catch fire and spread to other buildings on the grounds." Fortunately, the ongoing drizzle kept the embers from so spreading.

This was no ordinary building fire. The blaze was so spectacular that "hundreds of motorists parked their cars in the vicinity of the club to watch it," despite the inclement weather. The *Citizen* noted that "ribbon-like flames shot skyward for 30 feet, giving the appearance of lightning, differing however, as they retained visibility for several minutes. Another strange scene occurred when the blaze spread from the inside to the outside of the structure, igniting the siding [made of cedar] and boring the wood's grain, giving the appearance of a spider's web."

The spectators were further amazed when a "long, thin, whirlpool of flame shot skyward from the east end of the building." One of the firemen explained to an *Ohio State Journal* reporter that this phenomenon was a "fire fork," caused when "hot air sent into a whirlpool by air currents" is combined with combustible gases.

John Downey, having been snapped out of his supposed reverie at home by the unwelcome news, drove to the scene and watched the conflagration helplessly with Elks trustee George Pierce. The Elks' wonderful clubhouse was reduced to rubble, with only smoldering ruins and a fire-scarred chimney remaining. A pool table, some tables and chairs, an icebox and a few other miscellaneous items were all that could be salvaged. Gone was all the golf equipment stored in the ladies' locker room. Dr. John Walters, a guest of the

Golf in Columbus at Wyandot Country Club

club from New York (but who was not there at the time the fire broke out) lost his medical equipment.

There was much speculation about how the fire had started. A "short circuit in electric wiring or an overheated furnace spreading to kindling wood" piled too close to the furnace in the basement were being blamed as possible causes. John Downey loyally backed up his shaken caretaker, expressing "doubt that the fire had started from the furnace," as Timberlake had observed no fire when he was in the basement.

Reporters from the three Columbus newspapers, apprised that Downey was on the scene, pressed him for details on the resulting financial loss, the club's insurance coverage and what losing its clubhouse meant to the future of The Elks Country Club. He was able in large part to oblige them, because substantial information was reported in those papers the following day. He estimated losses at $100,000 for the clubhouse and $25,000 for its burned contents. The club carried insurance coverage in the amount of $75,000 on the building and $20,000 for its contents. Downey did his best to allay concerns that the fire might doom the course and club. He expected that The Elks' trustees would take steps toward construction of a new clubhouse. An emergency trustees meeting was scheduled for Tuesday to discuss the matter. Accordingly, the front-page headline in the November 3 edition of the *Columbus Citizen* assured readers, "Elks Plan to Rebuild House Swept by Fire."

But in reality, the trustees faced a difficult dilemma. Given that the clubhouse had been underinsured by at least $25,000, the construction of a new facility of the same scale as the one just lost meant that the BPOE would either have to cough up the difference from its own coffers or impose a special assessment on the members. Neither alternative was attractive. Wouldn't an assessment inevitably cause golfers to bolt to Brookside or York Temple, the hot new courses in town? Building a scaled-down clubhouse did not seem like the right answer either. Which of the amenities of the burned clubhouse could the club do without in a new building—the large lounging room, women's lockers, the dance hall, the grillroom, the full commercial kitchen or the sleeping rooms? Elimination of any of these facilities could markedly diminish The Elks' upper-tier "country club" brand.

Another big unknown was the question of how many members would resign during the winter simply because they did not want to wait around for construction of a new clubhouse. In that regard, the fire could not have come at a worse time. Typically, northern country club members who are on the fence about keeping their memberships choose to stay or leave in the month of November. Their reasoning for doing so is along the lines of:

The Elks Years, 1922-31

"Why postpone my decision? With the golf season over, I would rather not pay dues over the winter, when I do not intend to be using the club much anyway. I might as well leave now!" The destruction of the clubhouse was undoubtedly going to create a push toward resignation for some vacillating Elks members.

With all this uncertainty whirling about, and with so little time to digest the catastrophe, it is understandable that the trustees were not prepared to announce anything definitive after their meeting to discuss the club's predicament on November 4. But the BPOE's silence only served to ramp up the rumormongering. The most common whispering heard was that the Elks might dispose of the golf course. December and January passed, and still no definitive word had been conveyed to the anxious membership. By February, the number of dues payers had declined to 180 men and 50 women. Alarmed that the uncertainty of the situation might jeopardize The Elks' scheduled summer hosting of the Ohio Amateur, the Ohio Golf Association solicited proposals to host the tournament from other clubs.

Finally, the BPOE scheduled a meeting date of Wednesday, February 11, 1931, for its membership to consider a proposal from an unnamed prospective purchaser of its golf course. The entirety of the offer was not made public in advance of the meeting, but some details of the contemplated new operation were made known: (1) assuming the sale was agreed upon, the course would be "operated strictly for its golf features and not as a country club," and (2) the resulting club would be limited to private memberships.

The "founding father" most responsible for the golf course's creation was now about to become the "man of the hour" charged with the task of saving it.

PART II
The Wyandot Years, 1931–46

Chapter 10
FIRE SALE!

John W. Kaufman, sixty-four-year-old chairman of the board, and his fellow BPOE Lodge No. 37 trustees had regretfully concluded that the loss of the clubhouse, coupled with declining membership levels, rendered the lodge's retention of the golf course and property untenable. But how could the trustees obtain relief from this financial burden (let alone the expense of reconstructing the burned down clubhouse) while still ensuring that the 180 remaining golfing Elks could still play the golf course as members of a private club? An answer had to be found fast, or the unsettling lack of certainty could drive away the remaining golfers, the staff and the upcoming Ohio Amateur Championship.

Kaufman had personal reasons for wanting the course to survive. After all, it was he who had engineered the lodge's purchase of the 265-acre property, the building of its Donald Ross–designed golf course and the operation of its own country club. While a number of potential buyers expressed interest in purchasing the grounds, it is a good bet that Kaufman shuddered at the prospect that some fast-talking developer might wind up with the property and proceed to destroy the beautiful golf course he and his Elks had built. How could he help solve the BPOE's dilemma?

Kaufman was in the best position of anyone to effect the friendly bailout of the lodge and its golfers. Unlike most folks in 1931, the Kaufman family still had money. So, either at the behest of his fellow trustees or his own initiative, Kaufman decided to step up. He orchestrated an offer by the Glen Burn Company to purchase the entire club property from the BPOE. Glen

Golf in Columbus at Wyandot Country Club

Burn was a real estate partnership composed of John W., his son Harold and his son-in-law, Oscar "Dutch" Altmaier. John W. related the details of the transaction to the membership at the February 11 meeting of the lodge. He explained that Elks who were currently members of the soon-to-be-disbanded Elks Country Club would form a new golf club. Glen Burn, after taking ownership, would lease the property back to the new club for an indefinite period. John W. realized that finances would be tight for the fledgling club, so to assist it in getting off to a good start, "no rent would be charged for the first two years and then a nominal rent would be agreed upon which would allow the [newly formed] club to continue, as it [The Elks Country Club] has in the past, as a course where golfers of moderate means would not find dues beyond their reach."

John W. also formed an "organizing committee" of Elks members who would be entrusted with running the new club. The committee was to be headed by the affable green committee chairman, Tom Dempsey. He would become the new club's general manager. John W. also appointed Henry Watkins and J.F. Powers to the organizing committee. It might have seemed a bit unusual for landlord John W. to be the one appointing his new tenant's management team. However, it would have made no sense for him to go to the trouble of bailing his fellow Elks out of a financial jam unless he could be assured of excellent rapport with the new club's representatives.

Although John W. balked at having Glen Burn incur the expense of rebuilding the clubhouse, he proposed spending $15,000 on infrastructure improvements. These would include a new women's locker room, a new dining room adjacent to the present men's locker house and resurfacing the road leading to the locker room. Another $10,000 would be expended by Glen Burn on course improvements.

New man in charge, Tom Dempsey, provided additional details pertaining to the new club at the lodge meeting. He explained to the assemblage that a membership committee would be named to "restrict membership, although the new club is expected to absorb most of the members of the old Elks Country Club." The new club would not be restricted to the members of BPOE and would welcome applications from those outside the organization. The club would be operated solely as a golf club, with "no provision made for dances or any other kind of parties usually associated with a country club." The initiation fee would be set at a mere twenty-five dollars, with an annual membership fee in the amount of seventy-five dollars. The fees would be increased once the roster reached 200. The number of men's memberships would be closed once the number reached 250. Dempsey felt this number

The Wyandot Years, 1931–46

would be reached easily, "as most of the present membership is expected to remain and many local golfers who had been kept out by limitation to Elks members would now be recruited." Memberships for women would be available as well. Work on the improvements mentioned by Mr. Kaufman would start immediately. Dempsey also reassured attendees that professional Francis Marzolf, greenkeeper Lawrence Huber and locker room attendant Frank Whipp would continue in the service of the new club.

Dempsey advised that a new name for the club would be selected in the near future. The name would be "entirely divorced from either The Elks or Glen Burn, under which names the club has been designated in the past" (at no time in my research did I see the club or course referred to as "Glen Burn" until the Dempsey comments of February 11, 1931, were reported in the next day's newspapers). Dempsey reported that he had contacted the Ohio Golf Association and informed its officials that the new club would be ready for the Ohio Amateur "in plenty of time." Lawrence Huber had already manured the fairways, construction work had already been started and Dempsey was confident that the links "will be in better shape than ever during the coming year."

On February 23, the newly formed club announced its name. It would be called the Wyandot Golf and Country Club in honor of the "Indian tribe which formerly inhabited the region where the present Elks site is now located." Dempsey made no mention of "Last of the Wyandots" Bill Moose, often spotted at the club until old age finally caught up with the nonagenarian. Bill's infirmities had recently forced him out of his shack and into residence at the Franklin County Home. It had to cross the minds of the many who loved and admired Bill Moose that the course's new name should also be interpreted as a personal tribute to him. Certainly the image of the Native American on the scorecard bore a resemblance to old Bill.

Wyandot's new general manager, Dempsey, was extended good wishes by the *Citizen*'s sportswriter, Lew Byrer, who penned, "With Tom Dempsey, as fine a guy as Columbus golf knows, at its head, the new organization should prosper and become, in the future, an even greater factor in Columbus golf than in the past."

Dempsey and his fellow organizing committee member Henry Watkins were no doubt pleased to be working in harness together. The best friends played golf together two to three times weekly. Forever locked in a never-ending battle for bragging rights, the two high-80s shooters began keeping a cumulative tally of who had won more holes over their hundreds of matches. A Bill Needham–authored feature in the May 23, 1930 *Columbus*

Golf in Columbus at Wyandot Country Club

Above: Wyandot Country Club scorecard with its new insignia (note the "stymie gauge"). *Betty Huber collection.*

Left: Great pals Tom Dempsey and Henry Watkins. *From the Columbus Citizen, May 29, 1930.*

The Wyandot Years, 1931-46

Citizen indicated that Dempsey was currently holding a fifty-three-up lead after 12,762 holes! After each round, the winner of the day's match would proudly hang a red flag from his locker as a symbol of victory. Though it seems counterintuitive, each golf season's cumulative winner hosted the other fellow and his family for dinner.

Henry Watkins enjoyed telling the story of the fishing trip he took to Minnesota. Communication with the outside world from his remote camp was none too good. I'll let Henry take over the tale:

> *One day I received a telephone call from the telegram office. It was a wire from Dempsey. I asked the office to read it to me. "Went crazy and shot..." the girl read, and at that point the telephone wire broke down. I didn't know what sort of tragedy had happened to my friend. So I walked half a mile down the road to the closest phone to hear the rest of the telegram. It consisted of two words: "an 85."*

Dempsey plunged into the effort to recruit members for Wyandot. By March 27, he had succeeded in signing up 170 members. But he did not convince all the former Elks members to transfer their membership to Wyandot. He was unable to coax three key members of The Elks' golf team into the Wyandot fold. George Babcock, Max Matusoff and Eddie Hart had moved on. Even Johnny Florio considered playing his golf elsewhere. Melvin Carpenter, who had won the Columbus District Junior Championship under The Elks' banner, was gone, too, having joined the professional ranks.

These roadblocks caused Dempsey to redouble his membership drive efforts. One way to grab the attention of prospective members was to publicize the constant buzz of activity that Wyandot maintained throughout the spring. Construction of the new ladies' locker room and lounge moved along expeditiously. It was remarked in the *Dispatch*'s sports page that the ladies would have use of a facility "equipped with two marble shower rooms, four individual dressing rooms, with the floor of rose and blue tile."

The *Ohio State Journal*'s E.H. Peniston gave two thumbs up to the refurbished and reorganized men's locker room, noting that "twenty rooms will be provided, patterned after the Columbus Country Club. A table and six chairs will be found in each separate compartment." Peniston adjudged that "the new setup, modeled after Tom's idea, is great and a big improvement." Francis Marzolf's pro shop and the caddy master's station were redecorated also.

Improvements to the course were also in process. The ninth and eighteenth tees were elevated. Brush and trees to the right of the first

Golf in Columbus at Wyandot Country Club

The new locker room. *Columbus Memory, Scripps-Howard Newspapers/Grandview Heights Public Library/photo.org Collection.*

hole were eliminated. Peniston was wowed by the course's beauty that spring: "All the dogwood, red-bud, and other flowering trees and shrubs as well as the course, are at their best at Wyandot now, and worth a trip to see in themselves."

Another Dempsey brainchild was to place rakes (cheap ones to discourage theft) at each of Wyandot's 126 traps. Peniston approved of this new innovation and suggested that other Columbus courses follow suit because "it is a big help and doubtless helps cut down trap cussing to a minimum at Wyandot."

Dempsey and the rest of the Wyandot brain trust waited anxiously for word on whether the Ohio Golf Association would change the location of the Ohio Amateur scheduled for July 6. Having been spooked by the turmoil engulfing The Elks/Wyandot, the OGA required satisfaction that Dempsey and his team would have a well-maintained course and adequate facilities. Dempsey must have succeeded because on April 11, the OGA's secretary put an end to the speculation and announced that Wyandot would retain the championship. The OGA's F.S. Crooks mentioned that he would be meeting shortly with Dempsey to work out the plans for the event. It was definitely a major coup for Wyandot to become the first club to host the Ohio Open and Ohio Amateur in back-to-back years.

The Wyandot Years, 1931-46

Dempsey and company had to be delighted that Wyandot would be hosting the last leg of four spectacular golf events to be held in the Buckeye State during the period from June 19 to July 10, 1931. Preceding the state amateur would be (1) the prestigious Western Open at Miami Valley in Dayton, (2) the Ryder Cup team competition staged at Columbus's Scioto and (3) the U.S. Open, to be contested at Toledo's Inverness. Columbus golf fans and Wyandot members anticipated that local star and Elks alum Denny Shute would be inspired to play well in front of the home crowd at the Ryder Cup. Unfortunately, there was no guarantee Denny would make the team. He had failed to earn one of its automatic berths. But he would have one last opportunity to join the U.S. side. A seventy-two-hole qualifier would be contested at Scioto immediately prior to the start of Ryder Cup play. A committee of the PGA had selected thirteen players, including Denny, to fight it out for the final berths.

From all accounts, Denny Shute enjoyed the recognition he had earned in his adopted home of Columbus as its leading sports star and The Elks/Wyandot's favorite son. He also seemed happy with his affiliation at Brookside in Columbus, where he served as a co-professional with his father, Hermon. But those good feelings only made things more complicated when Lake Forest Country Club in Hudson, Ohio, 150 miles distant from Columbus, began romancing Denny in March 1931. The rumor circulated that Lake Forest had made him a very lucrative offer. The Hudson club supposedly had big plans—it was a major part of an ambitious real estate development that was just getting started. Luring a name like Denny to Lake Forest would certainly boost sales. Denny was apparently blown away by the club's promises, and he explored what seemed like a can't-miss opportunity. However, there was a fly in the ointment. Denny was still under contract to Brookside! Thus, on March 22, the *Ohio State Journal* reported, "Denny Shute will be back at Brookside, it was stated by Brookside officials Saturday. The rumor that he might go to Cleveland [which is near Hudson] is unfounded, for he has signed a contract to remain here."

There must have been some serious wheelin' and dealin' subsequent to March 22 because one week later, it was announced that Denny had accepted the Lake Forest job and would be leaving Columbus. Brookside had decided to let him go. The *Dispatch* piece noted that "Shute, now at Pinehurst, N.C. [competing in the North and South Open], wired J.S. McVey [Brookside club president] recently asking if he could be released from any contract, verbal or written, and the Brookside management replied that it was entirely up to Denny whether he wanted to remain in Columbus or go

Hermon and Denny Shute. *From the* Columbus Citizen, *May 29, 1933.*

elsewhere." McVey put the best face on Denny's departure from the club's perspective. He stated it would not be necessary to replace the sharpshooter because "Hermon Shute, who is now on the job, will handle the whole professional's burden at the club." The arrangement with Denny had been such that he had been allowed to spend most of his time away from the club in competitions anyway.

Before leaving town for good, Denny made the rounds in Columbus to say goodbye to his golfing friends. He expressed appreciation for the "marvelous treatment" he had received from Brookside officials and the Columbus public. He would have stayed in town, but Lake Forest had made him an offer he "did not feel he could refuse." The Elks/Wyandot's greatest golf alum probably wondered whether he would be well received by Columbus golf fans when he would soon mount his effort to qualify for the Ryder Cup

The Wyandot Years, 1931-46

at Scioto. If so, he needn't have worried. Denny would be warmly welcomed and still acclaimed as a "home boy" by everyone at the Ryder Cup.

Shute's departure was just one more indicator that "times were a-changin'" for the former Elks Country Club members. They were being solicited to join a much different club than the one they had been affiliated with in the Roaring Twenties. The big dances and formal social occasions held in the now-vanished clubhouse were all in the past. People with no BPOE connection would be joining. Wyandot was repositioning itself as a moderately priced golf-only club instead of competing with full-amenities upscale clubs like Scioto and Columbus. But eventually Dempsey was successful in persuading most of the old guard to join. Wyandot was working its way "out of the ashes" to a successful new beginning.

Johnny Florio overcame his reservations and signed up. Despite the loss of several regulars, any golf team featuring the one-two punch of Ohio Amateur champions Florio and Glen Bishop was going to be formidable. The Wyandot golf team showed it could still take on all comers in the *Ohio State Journal* team competition held on June 4 at Wyandot. The match with

The Wyandot clubhouse. *Columbus Memory, Scripps-Howard Newspapers/Grandview Heights Public Library/photo.org Collection.*

always-tough Scioto was deadlocked at 28 points when the final game of the day between Wyandot's W.E. Lynch and Scioto's Curtis Sohl reached the eighteenth. Realizing the outcome of the match rested on the shoulders of Messrs. Lynch and Sohl, members of both teams and other interested onlookers crowded behind the eighteenth green to cheer their boys. To the delight of the home faithful, Lynch's third shot from the rough crept close to the pin, thereby securing a thrilling Wyandot victory over its rival club.

This victory was the start of what would be an amazing stretch of golf for central Ohio golf fans and Wyandot's players in particular. First, Johnny Florio promptly followed up the team's big win by emerging victorious in the Central Ohio Amateur at Shawnee Country Club in Lima. Johnny had already enjoyed success in 1931 as a junior star on the George Sargent–coached Ohio State golf team and had won his way to the semifinals of the NCAA golf championship, where he was bested by OSU teammate Bob Kepler. He also managed to make the cut competing against the top tour pros in the Western Open. Given his good form and the fact that he would be competing on his home track, the scribes established Johnny as the clear favorite to stretch the amazing Elks/Wyandot string of Ohio Amateur wins to five straight.

But before the Amateur would be contested, there were two other golf events of global significance to take place in Ohio—the Ryder Cup at Scioto (preceded by the U.S team qualifier, in which Denny Shute would be participating) and the U.S. Open at Toledo's Inverness. What a smorgasbord of golf!

Chapter 11
THREE WEEKS

By June 1931, Elks product Denny Shute had certainly made a name for himself on the PGA tour. A player good enough to have won the Los Angeles and Texas Opens obviously had to be reckoned with. But his achievements to date left him a couple steps below the likes of Sarazen, Hagen and Armour. A good performance on the 1931 Ryder Cup's international stage at Scioto would go a long way toward further elevating Denny's status in the game. But first he had to make the team. That meant posting one of the four best scores in a special qualifier held during Ryder Cup week at Scioto. His fellow twelve competitors in the qualifier (picked by a PGA committee) included stars like Craig Wood, Billy Burke and Olin Dutra, all of whom would win major championships during their careers.

It might surprise golf aficionados to know that in these days of "captain's picks," a special qualifier was held and that U.S. captain Walter Hagen would not learn the identities of four of his 1931 team's members until shortly before the start of competition. And that 1931 qualifier proved to be the ultimate grind: seventy-two holes in two days in one-hundred-degree temperatures! Notwithstanding the heat, most of the players, including Denny, were attired in ties, long-sleeved shirts and plus fours. Wiffy Cox, Craig Wood and Billy Burke claimed three of the berths, but a three-way tie between Denny, Frank Walsh and Henry Ciuci for the final opening meant more golf for them. Despite the fact that foursome matches loomed on Friday, the PGA brass decreed that Shute, Walsh and Ciuci would decide things with another eighteen-hole playoff on Wednesday.

GOLF IN COLUMBUS AT WYANDOT COUNTRY CLUB

FINE WORK, THEY TELL DENNY

Top: Ciuci and Walsh congratulate Denny Shute or winning the final Ryder Cup position in a grueling playoff at Scioto. *Bottom*: Denny and Maddie celebrate Denny's making the U.S. Ryder Cup Team. *From the* Ohio State Journal, *June 26, 1931.*

The Wyandot Years, 1931-46

Ciuci faded early in Wednesday's withering cauldron and picked up on the par-three seventeenth. Denny birdied that same hole to wrest the lead by one from Walsh. On the eighteenth green, Walsh stood over a four-foot putt to tie Shute and force yet another eighteen-hole playoff on Thursday. He missed. Frank Walsh had lost the best opportunity he would ever have to play in the Ryder Cup. Denny had made the squad!

Things were not going well for the visitors even prior to Friday's foursomes. Three of their best players had been disqualified for trivial reasons. Henry Cotton committed the no-no of failing to sail over with the rest of the team. Cotton showed up at Scioto anyway but was relegated to playing an exhibition match with Bobby Jones. British stalwarts Aubrey Boomer and Percy Allis were also dinged for having golf club affiliations outside GB&I. To make matters worse, the Brits had difficulty coping with Columbus's blistering heat. There was also additional consternation generated by the PGA's decision to disallow the smaller ball approved for play outside the United States by the R&A.

Walter Hagen chose to take the exhausted Shute under his wing as his partner for the opening thirty-six-hole foursomes (alternate shot). When Denny confided to the captain that he was having some difficulty with fairway wood shots, Hagen arranged the batting order so that "The Haig" would be hitting the brassie, spoon and cleek second shots. Meshing perfectly, the two great match players trounced George Duncan and Arthur Havers, 10 and 9. Afterward, Hagen expressed pleasure with his rookie partner's steady golf, particularly given the fact that Denny was making his debut in the pressure cooker of the Ryder Cup. The *Citizen*'s Russ Needham pointed out that these were not idle words from The Haig for the benefit of a hometown boy as "he showed a few minutes later when he announced Shute would be in the lineup for the singles play Saturday and that the player to come out of the lineup was not Shute, or any of the other youngsters, but the veteran Leo Diegel, one of the four best golfers in the United States and present holder of the National P.G.A. championship."

Buoyed by the confidence placed in him by Sir Walter, Denny rolled to an 8 and 6 victory in his thirty-six-hole singles match against Bert Hodson. The United States took the Cup back stateside by a lopsided margin of 9 to 3. Denny Shute's first Ryder Cup experience, though exhausting, had been most rewarding. He emerged with two blowout victories and a big boost to his prestige. Moreover, any residual Columbus resentment prompted by Denny's move north dissipated in the glow of his success. Billy Burke also won his two matches. Both he and Denny headed to Inverness with momentum.

Golf in Columbus at Wyandot Country Club

Had Denny Shute complained about being subjected to an inordinately arduous qualifier, he would have received little sympathy from Burke and George Von Elm following their marathon battle at the following week's U.S. at Inverness. After seventy-two holes, Burke and Von Elm were deadlocked with scores of 292. The USGA rules then called for a thirty-six-hole playoff. Von Elm, the 1926 U.S. Amateur champion, birdied the last hole of that playoff to force another tie. The tie would be broken by—what else?—another thirty-six hole playoff! Finally, Burke nudged ahead and edged Von Elm by one stroke. After 144 holes, Billy Burke had finally won what would turn out to be his only major championship. He also became the first player to win the championship using steel-shafted clubs. Shute finished back in the pack at T-25.

Even before Von Elm and Burke had concluded their epic playoff, Wyandot was already busy hosting qualifying rounds for golfers attempting to earn their way into the state amateur field. A total of thirty-two survivors from the qualifier would compete at match play for the James Cox Trophy. The intense front-of-the-sports-page coverage provided by the *Columbus Evening Dispatch*, *Ohio State Journal* and *Columbus Citizen* suggests that local interest in the championship rivaled that exhibited for the Ryder Cup.

While all the members were excited that this prestigious event had been awarded to Wyandot, some expressed concern that the field might shoot embarrassingly low scores, given the course's relatively short length of 6,393 yards. Members of other clubs would sometimes refer to the course as a "Tom Thumb layout." Wyandot's Glen Bishop, the surprise state amateur champion of 1930, tackled this ticklish subject with the *Citizen*'s Russ Needham and sounded a warning: "There isn't a course in the country, I don't suppose, where care, precision, and variety is as necessary on tee shots as up at Wyandot. Two or three practice rounds on the course will be vitally necessary to get the peculiarities of the course well in mind. Even then a player, unless he stops and thinks each time he climbs up on a tee, is apt to get himself in unexpected trouble." Bishop predicted that "errors will be frequent and costly because on most courses the drive is just a mechanical swat with the art beginning from the second shot on."

The results of the thirty-six-hole qualifier were positively rapturous from the viewpoint of the Wyandot members. The course had proved surprisingly resistant to low scoring, A score of 164 had been good enough for match play—the highest qualifying total in memory! Scribe Needham got a kick out of the livid reactions of frustrated players who missed out: "Alibis flew around thicker than flies on a cherry pie. And the Wyandot members,

The Wyandot Years, 1931–46

congregated in one section of the locker room, listened and laughed. Wyandot may be short, but it surely isn't so sweet, except for the player who really hits his shots."

Not surprisingly, the medalist with a score of 143 was Wyandot's own Johnny Florio. Needham was already labeling the tournament as "more or less of a 'Johnny Florio state amateur.'" By conclusion of Tuesday's play, he had already won three awards: medalist honors, the driving contest (with an average of 265 yards on three blasts) and a shared prize with three other Wyandot members for having the best quartet of qualifying scores of any quartet of members hailing from the same club. But best of all, an astounding seven Wyandot members (22 percent of the competitors) would be taking part in match play. In addition to Johnny and Glen Bishop, other Wyandot qualifiers included Allen Tracewell, Norman Seidensticker, Frank Lewis, Austin Shannon and club champion Joe Outhwaite. Of the thirty-two total qualifiers, nineteen were affiliated with Columbus courses.

The match-play qualifiers were required to survive two matches on Wednesday. Florio won both of his games handily with 5 and 4 victories. Lewis, Bishop and Seidensticker made it to the afternoon round of sixteen. But then Bishop was dethroned in extra holes. Seidensticker scored an upset win over former Columbus District champion Raleigh Lee. Lewis, however, was annihilated by Florio's Ohio State teammate Bob Kepler, 8 and 7. If there was a second betting favorite behind Johnny, it would have been his teammate Kepler. Still in excellent form after making it to the finals of the NCAA tournament, as well as a victory in the Columbus District tournament, he was poised to make a strong challenge.

It is possible that Johnny might have been looking ahead when he faced fellow member Norman Seidensticker in the quarterfinals. Norman, a former Notre Dame golf team captain and Columbus District medalist, gave Florio an unexpected scare. The match lasted to eighteen, with Florio escaping unscathed with a one-up triumph.

Florio would then face James "Scotty" Reston of Dayton in the semis. Reston had just been named the captain of the golf team at the University of Illinois, where he was studying journalism. Scotty had demonstrated early aptitude for golf and had previously won Ohio's 1927 high school championship. He was spending his summer employed as the starter at another Clintonville course, Indian Springs. Coincidentally, Reston knew well the namesake for the championship trophy, newspaper publisher and former Ohio governor James Cox, having frequently caddied for him at the Dayton Country Club.

GOLF IN COLUMBUS AT WYANDOT COUNTRY CLUB

James "Scotty" Reston (left) and Bob Kepler, finalists in the 1931 Ohio Amateur held at Wyandot. *From the* Columbus Evening Dispatch, *July 11, 1931.*

Johnny had already defeated Reston in the NCAA tournament, so it was no surprise when Florio quickly gained the upper hand in their semifinal match. He held a two-up lead after six holes after canning a birdie on the sixth hole. But Reston's spectacular play on Wyandot's back nine turned the match around. By the time the players reached the sixteenth, Florio was one down. When Johnny's tying six-footer stayed out, Reston was dormie. After the seventeenth was halved with pars, Johnny had been eliminated, 2 and 1. Kepler advanced to the final with a taut one-up victory over Arlington's Theron Green. Kepler's brilliant second shot to the green on eighteen clinched the hole and the match.

The thirty-six-hole final pitted two Western Conference (forerunner to the Big 10) foes and Dayton natives. They had met twice before in high school and Dayton district play, splitting the two matches. Kepler got off to a decidedly inauspicious start, badly hooking his tee shot on the first hole. The ball bounced off a tree and into the ravine. After seven holes, Reston

The Wyandot Years, 1931-46

enjoyed a three-up advantage. But then Reston lost the par-three eighth to Kepler's par. Bob capitalized on the opening with birdies on ten and eleven to square the match. By lunch, he enjoyed a one-up lead. By the afternoon's seventh hole, Reston had fallen three down. But then Kepler faltered with bogies on eight and nine. Scotty emerged only one hole down at the turn. But, as Glen Bishop had prognosticated, poor tee shots were the difference in the match. Hooked tee shots on ten and twelve cost Reston two holes he could ill afford to lose. His badly topped brassie second shot on fifteen gutted any lingering hope of recovery. Kepler had won the match and the championship, 4 and 3.

Despite the fact that its string of Ohio Amateur champions had been snapped, it had been a superlative week for Wyandot and its members. The course had proven to be a great test of golf. Players who consistently hit accurate tee shots scored well. But foolishly smashing the driver when a cleek would have been the more prudent choice caused the scores of many of Ohio's best to balloon. Russ Needham summed up: "It's a tricky course where scores may be either very low or amazingly high. But it abounds in interesting holes. And its scenery is delightful."

What happened to the two finalists, Bob Kepler and Scotty Reston? Their lives traveled down very different paths. Kepler became the golf coach at Ohio State University. He enjoyed a long tenure there (only one year less than that of Woody Hayes) from 1938 to 1965. He coached the team to the 1945 NCAA championship and mentored great players like Johnny Lorms, Tom Nieporte (both individual NCAA champions) and Tom Weiskopf. But he will forever be remembered as Jack Nicklaus's college coach. Under Kepler's guidance, Jack twice won the NCAA championship. Jack also gives credit to Kepler for teaching him how to fish. But as we have seen, Kepler could play a little golf, too!

The other finalist capitalized on his association with James Cox. After college, Scotty was hired by the *Dayton Daily News*, a Cox-owned newspaper. After a brief sojourn in public relations with Ohio State and the Cincinnati Reds, Scotty landed a job with the Associated Press in New York City. From 1937 to 1939, he was stationed in London, where he covered the Nazi blitz of that city for AP. After a stellar performance in that post, Reston joined the *New York Times* and was transferred to the paper's Washington bureau. Ultimately, he was given his own column. Before he was finished, he would interview eight presidents and receive two Pulitzer Prizes for journalism. James Reston became one of the most influential journalists of his era.

Chapter 12
THE END OF A GREAT ELK

Sad tidings arrived at the Elks Home at 256 East Broad Street on Sunday, October 1, 1933. John W. Kaufman, age sixty-six, had passed away at Otis Hospital in Celina, Ohio. He had taken ill while vacationing at the family summer home on Lake St. Mary's. He had been suffering for five weeks with "inflammation of the liver, following an attack of intestinal influenza." The *Dispatch* obituary indicated that Mr. Kaufman was survived by his wife, Elizabeth Wagner Kaufman; his son, Harold J. Kaufman; and daughters Margaret Kaufman Kirby and Mary K. Altmaier. John W. also left nine surviving siblings—five brothers and four sisters. Largely through his entrepreneurial efforts, many in this large extended family spent their careers in good positions with various businesses that John W. acquired, built or founded. Funeral services were scheduled for Wednesday at Kaufman's home at 1151 Bryden Road.

The obituary summed up Kaufman's involvement with The Elks/Wyandot this way: "It was through his help that The Elks Country Club was financed and built north of Columbus, and it was he [as the driving force in Glen Burn] who purchased it from the lodge and maintained it as the Wyandot Country Club when a difficult financial situation developed."

From what we know of him, it does not appear that Mr. Kaufman's extraordinary efforts to make The Elks and Wyandot clubs and its classic Ross-designed golf course a reality were motivated much by love of golf. They were prompted more by his intense desire that his brothers in Elks Lodge No. 37 have the best of everything. Throughout his adult life, John

The Wyandot Years, 1931-46

W. had expended his time and treasure of behalf of the BPOE, had been its chief fundraiser and had filled every important capacity in the local lodge. He was still serving in the post of grand trustee of the National Lodge of Elks when he died. Though perhaps uncommon for an obituary to reference a deceased as a beloved "clubman," it was a fitting appellation for John W. Kaufman.

But doing good for the Elks was not Kaufman's only avocation. He became an inveterate visitor to the western United States and Canada. As he aged, he increasingly indulged his passion for travel to the "Wild West," and his journeys became longer and more frequent. In 1925, he planned his most ambitious western excursion. He and six fellow Elks would caravan a small bus and truck westward for fourteen weeks of camping. Other than a few nights in hotels in Los Angeles and Portland (the latter city was the site of the BPOE convention, which the "Roving Brothers" attended), the boys camped every night. While there were no attacks by Indians or outlaws to fear, the West was still relatively untamed in 1925. Roads were treacherous and often washed out. The vehicles often broke down. Supplies and provisions were not always easy to come by. Rivers needed to be ferried. Public camps were only occasionally available, and bathing was a sometime thing.

The trip received a significant amount of publicity, and Kaufman decided to compile a memoir of the journey. Normally modest, he expressed the view that he and his Elks brothers had taken "the most entertaining and fascinating tour of the West ever chronicled in modern history." *Legends of the Roving Brothers* (a copy of which I managed to acquire via E-bay) is an amazingly professional and artistic publication. The brown-tinted text and photographs on heavy stock paper with a weathered appearance evoke the feel of roughing it out west. The photographs of the landscapes contained in the journal are staggering in their Ansel Adams–like clarity. Even well-drawn cartoons made their way into the story, such as the one featuring Kaufman ("The Skipper").

Kaufman and his fellow travelers gave each other nicknames for the trip. "The Dish Washer," "The Baler," "The Produce Buyer," "The Maid," "The Pilot," "The Cook," "The Cowboy" and, of course, Kaufman's "The Skipper" were generally descriptive of the functions and chores each performed in the daily life of the camp.

From Big Springs, Nebraska, and Hidden River, Wyoming, to Gardiner, Montana, and Indian Massacre Rocks, Idaho, and then on to the grandeur of the Columbia Highway and Rainier, Oregon, the "Roving Brothers" roamed. The band of brothers made sure to chronicle each day's activities

Road near Shoshone Falls. *From* Legends of the Roving Brothers, *by John W. Kaufman.*

Opposite: John W. Kaufman, "The Skipper." *From* Legends of the Roving Brothers, *by John W. Kaufman.*

The Wyandot Years, 1931-46

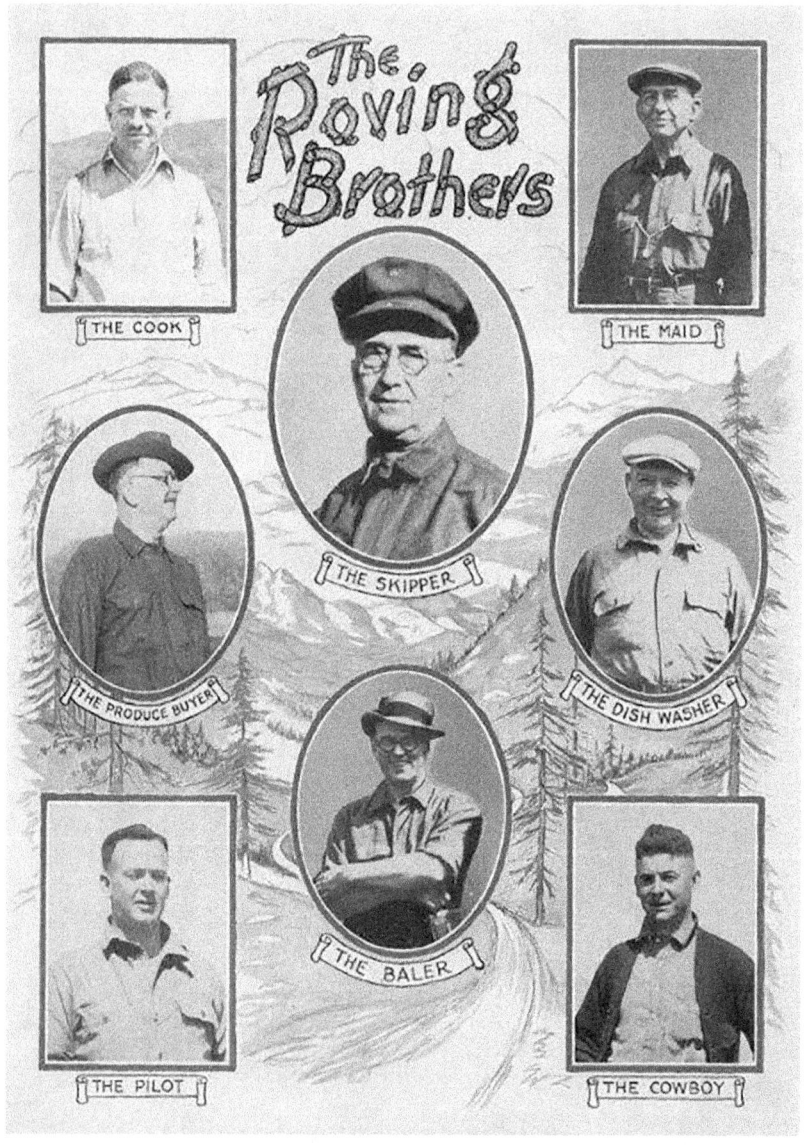

The Roving Brothers. *From* Legends of the Roving Brothers, *by John W. Kaufman.*

for the journal. Most were written in a lighthearted, breezy style that pooh-poohed the hardships and hazards they experienced. Kaufman relished meeting the daily challenges in the company of his fellow Elks. In acknowledgement of appreciation to his bunkmates, he wrote:

The Wyandot Years, 1931-46

Humor, wit, conviviality,
never lagging-
No task too arduous,
No duty too severe
Ever faithful and loyal
Keen to do their bit
With shovel and pick
In sunshine and rain
No sands too deep, no grades too steep

On their way back east, the Roving Brothers hit several of the stops later memorialized in the song "Route 66": Barstow, California; Kingman and Flagstaff, Arizona; and Gallup, New Mexico. Many of the roads were dirt paths not greatly improved from the covered wagon days. Finally, on September 30, 1925, the crew approached Columbus. The journal reports that the boys were "in more or less a pensive mood" as they crossed the state line back into Ohio. Most were sorry the trip was ending. The last "Gilded Camp" was the Deshler Hotel at the northwest corner of Broad and High. A few of the Roving Brothers came from northern Ohio and thus would be spending the night at the Deshler.

Still in camp fatigues, the weary travelers made their way to the Elks Home at 256 East Broad Street. According to the journal, "the ovation accorded the skipper [Kaufman] is beyond words. Approximately 400 members were present…It was a glorious meeting in every detail, the finest Elks chorus in America sang several selections. There were speeches of welcome and so on, a flashlight picture; but it would have warmed your heart could you have heard our Skipper unlimber. The rigors of camp life not only made him fit physically, but mentally as well. Words flowed from his mouth like ripples in a brook. There was nothing in the vocabulary that did not occur to him. Not too much, not too little, but just enough to be thoroughly effective."

Glen Rohn, "The Baler," composed an admiring tribute to John W. Kaufman in the last entry of *Legends of the Roving Brothers*. Coincidentally, it was written and dated October 1, 1925—exactly eight years to the day prior to John W. Kaufman's death. If Rohn's reflections about "The Skipper" had been repeated word for word at the funeral, they would have made for a perfect eulogy:

A character of unusual forcefulness, willing to act and serve, quick to grasp any situation, compassionate, ever ready to forgive, fearless in the face of danger, with grit and stamina enough for a dozen men, kindly, chivalrous, hospitable, John Kaufman is all of the traditional southern hospitality rolled into one composite character, standing apart from the world. It is customary that we ignore the living and eulogize the dead. But it seems to me that when there exists such a human being, placed in this untoward world ostensibly to make it a better place in which to live, a word of him at this time is not out or order. For the first time, this letter goes forth without being submitted to his censorship, for he is pleasingly modest, extremely so about matters of this kind, and would not, under any circumstances, sanction or consent to this slight tribute to the nobleness of his character...And I know full well the other members of the Roving Brothers take the same stand with me. Majority rules. Quite so!

The Baler went on to say that the disbanding of the Roving Brothers "naturally makes us wistful; there is a tear in our eye, a lump in our throat and sadness grips our heart." No doubt all of those sentiments were similarly expressed at John W. Kaufman's funeral.

The greatest friend of the Wyandot Country Club was gone. In the aftermath of Kaufman's demise, many members must have contemplated whether the passing of this "Great Elk" would affect the club's relationship with Glen Burn, Wyandot's landlord.

Chapter 13
LADIES FIRST

Wyandot's professional, Francis Marzolf, knew she was something special as soon he started giving her lessons. She was extremely erratic, but man could she ever murder a driver! Right from the beginning, Isabel Emmons's natural athleticism enabled her to blast her tee shots past most of the male players at Wyandot. According to Marzolf, her drives would travel 215 to 250 yards. Much like Babe Didrikson, she excelled at all athletic endeavors. Isabel's best skill was tennis (she had won the city championship), but once she committed to golf, the other sports fell by the wayside. The *Citizen*'s Lew Byrer happened to be visiting Marzolf just after he took over the club pro job at The Elks. Isabel was not yet breaking 100 consistently, but the pro had observed sufficient talent that he mentioned to Byrer, "I've a woman pupil up here who is going to be heard from in tournament circles. She has the distance right now and her accuracy is improving. And—best of all—she loves to play and loves to practice."

And how! Once hooked on the game, Mrs. Emmons could be found at Wyandot every day that it was playable. Often, she played thirty-six holes. She obtained frequent lessons from Marzolf and supplemented those with tutelage from Charlie Lorms at Columbus Country Club. As Marzolf had foretold, her game skyrocketed. By 1930, only her second year of golf, Mrs. Thornton Emmons (like most women of that era, Isabel used her husband's name in competition) posed a legitimate threat to win the local championship. She made the final of the women's Franklin County Amateur that year before bowing to Mrs. Curtis (Blanche) Sohl, playing out of Scioto.

GOLF IN COLUMBUS AT WYANDOT COUNTRY CLUB

The fashionable ladies of Wyandot Country Club. *From the* Columbus Citizen, *July 16, 1932.*

Isabel made another run at the Franklin County event in 1931 before being turned away again by Mrs. Sohl in the quarterfinals.

The Elks/Wyandot had earned the label "Maker of Champions" due to the sensational string of Ohio Amateur titles earned by its crack male stars from 1927 to 1932. The dominance of the Wyandot men waned after Johnny Florio's 1932 Ohio Amateur victory. But the Wyandot women, led by Mrs. Emmons, immediately began picking up the slack with their dazzling performances.

Mrs. Emmons raised her game several notches by lapping the field when she equaled Columbus Country Club's women's par of 81 in the qualifying round of the 1932 Franklin County Amateur. Finishing a very distant second was her archrival Mrs. Sohl, who carded an 89. Isabel's form held through to the final, where she confronted Blanche Sohl once again. This time Isabel turned the tables. Outdriving Sohl by twenty-five to forty yards, she never trailed. She closed out the final 3 and 2 by canning a twenty-foot birdie putt on the sixteenth.

The Wyandot Years, 1931–46

Mrs. Emmons decided in 1933 to make her debut in the state amateur at Akron's Portage Country Club. The blond, curly haired wife and mother of two raised eyebrows by taking out Mrs. Sohl, the 1929 champion, in the second round. Mrs. Emmons followed up that victory by knocking off defending champion Mrs. Larry Nelson in the quarterfinal match. After dusting off Mrs. Hoyt Smith in the semis, she faced Mrs. Linton Fallis of Toledo in the final.

The thirty-six-hole final match was a tense affair chock-full of drama. In an early hole, a controversy ensued. Mrs. Emmons's caddy followed her into a bunker and then set her golf bag down on the sand. Convinced that this was an infraction, Mrs. Emmons called a penalty on herself, which Mrs. Fallis refused to accept. An official was called, and ruled there was no penalty. Mrs. Emmons did not argue but intentionally took the wrong club out of the bunker and sent the ball far across the green, effectively assessing the penalty stroke she felt she was required to take.

Mrs. Thornton Emmons, 1933 Women's State Amateur champion. *From the* Columbus Citizen, *May 29, 1930.*

The lead seesawed back and forth all day, with Mrs. Fallis's fantastic putting compensating for comparatively short hitting. On the thirty-fifth hole, the feisty Mrs. Fallis's par three catapulted her into a one-up dormie lead. Mrs. Emmons heroically responded with a high-pressure brassie shot to within twelve feet of the thirty-sixth hole to square the match.

Then it was on to the first hole (and the thirty-seventh of the match)! Having to play this hole for everything caused Mrs. Emmons great consternation. She was superstitious, you see, and apparently thought it a bad omen to win the first hole. Twice during the week, she had intentionally missed putts to lose the first.

Golf in Columbus at Wyandot Country Club

She overcame this unusual phobia by splitting the fairway with her "rifle-like" long drive and then striking a smooth mashie-niblick fifteen feet from the pin. Her resulting par was good enough to take the title. Mrs. Thornton Emmons had won the Ohio State Amateur in only her fifth year of playing golf.

Afterward, the press expressed bemusement at Mrs. Emmons's approach to tournament golf. She didn't particularly like it. It was way too serious—she felt the game should be fun. Isabel preferred playing casual rounds with her husband or friends. Lew Byrer commented, "I'm not sure she isn't right. For golf, after all, is played for the love of the thing. And tournament players I have watched seldom seem to be having much fun."

Mrs. Emmons repeated her Franklin County Amateur triumph in 1934. In an amazingly brief period of time, she had shot past her Franklin County rivals to become the undisputed queen of Columbus golf. Only thirty-five years old, it seemed certain that Isabel would dominate the women's golf scene for another two decades. She wasn't the only excellent Wyandot female player. Young Sally Elson and Miss Chester (yes, that was her given name, not her husband's) Skees were beginning to make their marks. Perhaps operating under the "if you can't beat 'em, join 'em" theory, Mrs. Sohl also joined Wyandot. Surely, Emmons, Sohl, Elson and Skees would form an unbeatable quartet in club team play for years to come.

Shortly after New Year's Day 1935, Mrs. Emmons became ill. She came down with pneumonia, and without the antibiotics administered today to combat the illness, her condition suddenly became grave. She succumbed to the illness on January 15, leaving behind her husband, Thornton, a vice-president with American Zinc Sales Co., and their children, Virginia and George. Her passing made front-page news. The *Journal*'s E.H. Peniston penned the following emotional homage:

> *It is a calamity when any city loses its best woman athlete, as did Columbus when it lost Mrs. Thornton Emmons, Monday. But it is a stark tragedy when it loses a woman whose sportsmanship was even more outstanding than was her ability as an athlete. It is easy enough to say of one who has passed on that he or she was the community's best sportsman or sportswoman. Nobody will dispute it then. But I know that if one had asked any woman golfer in Columbus last week or last month or last year who was our foremost sportswoman, they would have as unhesitatingly answered "Isabel Emmons"....A city can replant a tree which has fallen before a hurricane. It cannot replant examples of sportsmanship. They are born, not made. They come but once, perhaps, in many generations.*

The Wyandot Years, 1931-46

Sorrowful over the loss of their friend and leader, the Wyandot women evidently determined that the best way to honor Isabel's legacy would be to rack up more tournament wins for Wyandot. The petite, comely Miss Elson kept the county amateur in the club's hands when she won the title for the first time in 1935. In '36, Sally, Blanche and Chester made it three Wyandot golfers out of four in the semis of that year's county championship, held at Columbus Country Club. Skees took down Elson one-up to advance to the final against Blanche Sohl. Mrs. Sohl won the title for the seventh time with a 4-and-3 triumph. Sally consoled herself by setting the women's course record at Wyandot in September with a 75. It could have been an even better round, but she took 6 on the easy seventeenth. She built on that achievement by rebounding to win the county title in 1937.

Sally Elson (left) and Blanche Sohl. *From the* Columbus Citizen, *June 23, 1936.*

Golf in Columbus at Wyandot Country Club

Led by Sally, along with additional reinforcements Mrs. Parker La Moore, Mrs. A.W. Simpson and Mrs. A. Ward Sumpter, the Wyandot women's contingent descended upon Scioto to compete in the 1937 Ohio State Amateur. In addition to striving for individual honors, the club's women wanted to win the Citizen's Trophy, which would be awarded to the club whose four players scored the lowest gross aggregate in the qualifying round. It was no surprise when the Wyandot women swept this team competition.

Sally, enjoying a blazing hot streak, marched her way into the finals against Miss Isabel Ogilvie of Cleveland. Before the match, Miss Elson placed a four-leaf clover in one of her shoes. However, this seemed to backfire, as she suffered the bad luck of being victimized by several stymies. The normally effervescent Miss Elson kept a poker face as momentum in the thirty-six-hole final shifted first toward Miss Ogilvie and then back to Sally.

Finally, on Scioto's eleventh (the twenty-ninth of the match), Sally, employing her "Mills head" wooden-shafted putter, stroked a putt for birdie from thirty feet. When it dropped, she broke out in "a smile as wide as the Grand Canyon from ear to ear." She followed that bomb with another fifteen-footer on number twelve to win that hole as well. She ran out the match 4 and 3. Interviewed thereafter, Sally confided, "I felt then [after the thirty-footer on eleven] that I was going to win the match. That putt bothered Isabel and gave me back my courage."

The women's terrific play in the '30s rivaled the achievements of the Elks' men in the "Golden Era" from '27 to '32. While the women did not win any more state titles, one of them received a special honor. Blanche Sohl, now a golf instructor in Ohio State's athletic department, was invited along with OSU coach Bob Kepler to play the May 18, 1940 opening round at the dedication for OSU's two new golf courses. Filling out the day's foursome would be golf legends Chick Evans and Patty Berg. As was nearly always the case for the esteemed Wyandot women of the 1930s, Mrs. Sohl acquitted herself well in the heady presence of great players.

In her capacity as an OSU instructor, Mrs. Sohl did such a bang-up job teaching one young woman the game that the pupil became a regular on the Ohio State women's golf team. That Buckeye team won the third Women's National Collegiate Championship in 1947. The student in question was Ellen Marzolf (yes, Francis's daughter). Maybe because she had the game all around her growing up, Ellen resisted playing until signing up for Mrs. Sohl's golf class. Blanche's imparted wisdom propelled Ellen Marzolf Hallerman into a lifetime love of golf.

Chapter 14
FUN TIMES

As he had done hundreds of times, Johnny Florio eyed his impending tee shot on Wyandot's rather claustrophobic first hole. The 403-yard par four presented such a severe dogleg left that a hitter of Johnny's length would normally club down to a spoon (three wood) or cleek (four wood) to keep from driving through the fairway into the trees on the right. Wyandot's professional, Francis Marzolf, the man who had selected Johnny to find the fairway on the course's scariest tee shot, looked on with full confidence that he had made the correct choice. After all, Johnny Florio had been the victor in the 1932 Ohio Amateur championship the previous summer at Akron's Portage Country Club.

In order to save every millisecond, Marzolf instructed Johnny to start his backswing the moment that official timer (and Columbus Redbirds baseball team president) George Trautman gave the signal that the "Great Relay Race" was underway. Francis had organized what was sure to be a chaotic relay race in order to publicize the club and hopefully attract some new members. How fast could a round of golf be played by twenty-five of the club's members by positioning them so there would always be someone ready to strike the next shot the moment the previous one came to rest? Once a golfer played the shot, he or she would be hustled by automobile to play another shot on a subsequent hole. The ball was to be relayed in this fashion from shot to shot and hole to hole. In masterminding this mêlée, Francis figured that in addition to playing speedily, his golfers needed to play well. Time wasted searching for balls in the woods would doom the relay team's

Golf in Columbus at Wyandot Country Club

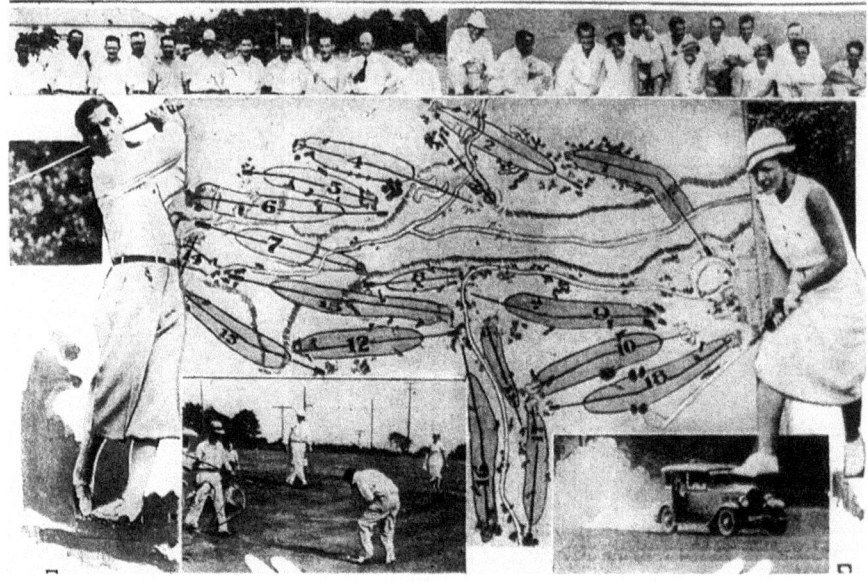

(Top) The twenty-five Wyandot players who participated in the "Great Relay Race"; (left) Johnny Florio driving off number one; (right) Mrs. Thornton Emmons putting out on number nine; (bottom left) Glen Bishop holes final putt on number eighteen; (bottom right) Tom Dempsey's automobile careens around a bunker to deliver Mrs. Emmons to the ninth green. *From the* Columbus Citizen, *July 23, 1933.*

effort. Thus, he would station his best players—Johnny, Glen Bishop, Mrs. Thornton Emmons and southpaw state champ E.G. Livesay—in position to hit the treacherous shots where misses would be the most time-costly.

So when George Trautman hit the stopwatch and yelled, "Go!" Johnny Florio swung into action. However, at the top of Johnny's backswing, the game plan, so carefully thought out by Marzolf, went awry. Sportswriter Lew Byrer had been delegated the task of firing a shot to alert the other relay team members that the race had begun. Unaccountably, he pulled the trigger in Florio's mid-swing, and the resounding discharge caused Johnny to flinch and snipe-hook his ball deep into the woods. With the clock ticking, Johnny had no choice but to re-tee. This effort was better, but a precious twenty seconds or so had been irretrievably lost.

The second hole featured an even worse comedy of errors. Glen Bishop, 1930 state amateur champion, pushed his drive badly into the ravine. Mr. Thornton Emmons, poised to hit the second shot, mistakenly thought that the ball had entered the ravine close to the tee, so he began sprinting back

The Wyandot Years, 1931–46

toward Bishop. Glen, realizing that Thornton was confused, began running to where he believed the ball had disappeared. In their mutual anxiety, the two actually passed each other. Emmons finally found the ball and hurriedly made a poor shot just 50 yards ahead. Fortunately, the miss stopped right at Bishop's feet, from which he remarkably hit his driver (still in his hand) off the deck to the edge of the green. Another mix-up occurred on the fourth hole when nobody showed up to hit the second shot. Bishop, riding by en route to the fifth tee, jumped out of a car driven by Tom Dempsey and played a fine spoon to the green. With Bishop now unavailable, Dempsey sped to the fifth tee with only his putter in tow. After Mrs. Emmons holed out on four, Tom improvised brilliantly by smashing his "putt" 170 yards down the fifth fairway.

From there, all proceeded more or less according to plan until the tenth tee. Livesay was late in arriving, so L.W. St. John, Ohio State University's athletic director (and the namesake for OSU's St. John Arena), grabbed a brassie and smacked a great shot down the middle.

Briefly, the team got on a roll. Don Dutcher rolled home a fifteen-foot birdie putt on twelve, and Bill Hinchman chipped in for another bird on thirteen. Whether it was the blood rushing to his head after that sensational chip, his mad dash to the fourteenth tee or the fact that Marzolf was impatiently waiting to play the next shot (hopefully a putt), Hinchman made a mess of things by promptly dumping two balls in the water on the short, picturesque par three. Then, on fifteen, Mrs. Emmons putted the ball before it had stopped rolling, resulting in a four-putt. One final snafu involving the club's two best players closed the round. Florio's second shot on the home hole finished off to the right and behind Dempsey's automobile, which had brought Bishop to the green ostensibly to hole the final putt. Now in full Keystone Cops panic mode, Bishop struck his pitch before Dempsey had cleared the car from the path of the shot. The ball banged into the vehicle and was hanging on the running board as Dempsey was driving away. It finally dropped off, and Glen ultimately holed out in seven. Whew!

Despite several hilarious miscues, the Wyandot players had established a new relay world record, having completed the circuit in twenty minutes and forty-one seconds and carding a credible 89 in the process (according to the Internet, the current golf relay world record is in the neighborhood of eight minutes). This madcap event made the first page of the *Citizen*'s sports section on July 23, 1933, and was widely reported outside Ohio.

The club devised other thoughtful ways of furthering camaraderie among the members and enriching the golfing experience. Members living in Delaware formed a team to play competitive matches against residents of other surrounding communities. Another brainstorm involved a match between the two sides of the men's locker room, with the losing side buying dinner. Wyandot's treasurer, Bill Margraf, inaugurated a third new event—the "Board of Directors' 72-Hole Medal Play Handicap Tournament," designed to encourage more members to play in competition. It was contested over four successive weekends. The entrants were given the choice of playing their tournament round either Saturday or Sunday of each weekend, provided they designate in advance which day's round was to count as the tournament score.

Margraf did not have far to travel when visiting the club. His home was located adjacent to the third fairway. It seems that Bill must have been engaged in a golf course romance because he married one of the club's female members and best players, Chester Skees. They formed a formidable duo in the mixed competitions. The Margrafs once teamed to shoot a gross score of 74 in the alternate-shot format. Bill, a single-digit handicapper, also contributed to Wyandot's men's team's ongoing success in interclub completion. His service on the board was also of great benefit to the club. He was a confidant of the Kaufmans, having managed a Marble Cliff Quarry division for a number of years. Bill ultimately made a career in golf. He served with distinction for twenty years as the executive secretary of the Ohio Golf Association, responsible for organizing the important statewide events. As a posthumous tribute to Margraf and his wife, the local Columbus District Golf Association conducted a mixed event called The Margraf for many years.

But Bill Margraf's greatest contribution to Wyandot lore was his pleasing singing voice. Teamed with friends Stark Frambes Jr. and Pat Crowe, Bill headed up an unforgettable musical trio at the "19th hole." Given the picture Russ Needham of the *Dispatch* painted of the post-round Wyandot locker room, it could have passed for the set of a Hollywood musical:

> *Crowe played the guitar, Frambes the uke or mandolin, Margraf could sing tenor, baritone, or bass as the occasion demanded. In from a round of golf, they'd start, "I Want a Girl," "Down by the Old Mill Stream," "When You Were a Tulip," "There's a Long, Long Trail" and all the others each got their evening workout. Those who were in the locker room before joined in, and so did the others as they filed in off the course. Some might be in the showers, others shaving, but the songs went on. It was one huge choral society.*

THE WYANDOT YEARS, 1931-46

The Locker Room Singers featuring Bill Margraf on the guitar. *From the* Columbus Evening Dispatch, *May 24, 1936.*

Like Bill Margraf, former South High coach Herb Bash also made his living in the golf industry. Herb and his wife owned the Berwick Golf Course, a public facility located on the city's southeast side. Herb helped grow the game at Berwick by conducting numerous golf clinics for the city's youths. Shortly after joining The Elks in 1928, Bash, in partnership with Bugs Raymond, opened another golf course—Indian Springs, opposite Henderson Road on the east side of High Street. Herb later added the Bash Driving Range in Dublin to his collection of entrepreneurial golf activities. Like many of his compatriots at The Elks/Wyandot, Herb Bash could golf his ball. Prior to joining The Elks, he won Dublin Road's club championship. Herb was also a mainstay of the 1932 Wyandot golf team, which won the interclub championship.

There were myriad competitive outlets for Wyandot's better players in the '30s. The Columbus Citizen's Private Golf League, established in 1936, featured interclub matches every third Sunday. The eight-man teams hailed from Scioto, York, Brookside, Columbus, Granville and Wyandot. The *Citizen*

GOLF IN COLUMBUS AT WYANDOT COUNTRY CLUB

INDIAN SPRINGS

HERB BASH

Herb Bash. *From the* Columbus Citizen, *June 2, 1936.*

awarded a trophy each year to the league's champion. The Columbus Golf League provided another battleground for good club players. The KingTaste Products team was a perennial champion. Johnny Florio was one of the league's all-stars.

In 1932, Wyandot served as the home course for the Ohio State Buckeyes. OSU's athletic director, Lynn St. John, a valued Wyandot member, was instrumental in orchestrating this arrangement. St. John also named Francis Marzolf the team's coach that year, succeeding George Sargent. Johnny Florio, now twenty-three, was still a varsity player, so Wyandot members were provided an opportunity to cheer their favorite son in Western Conference action. Unfortunately, depleted finances forced OSU to temporarily suspend the golf team's activities in 1933, and the golf team drifted away from the club.

Not every member was a star golfer. Cy Watkins was perhaps more typical. Cy had no time for golf as a young man, having been immersed in building his business, the Watkins Printing Company. In his forties, Cy's business interests had progressed to the point where he finally could afford some leisure time. He took up golf, enjoyed it and joined Wyandot. However, Cy started golfing a little too late in life to develop into a first-class player. The same could not be said for his teenage son Dwight. The young boy took full advantage of the opportunity the course provided, playing and caddying whenever possible. After Wyandot closed down, both father and son joined Brookside. Son Dwight raised his game to a level good enough to win Brookside's club championship! At age eighty-eight, Dwight still consistently shoots under his age. When he outdistances his

THE WYANDOT YEARS, 1931–46

Coach Francis Marzolf (second from left) with his 1932 Ohio State golf team. Bob Kepler (third from right) and Johnny Florio (far right) join him. *Ellen Marzolf Hallerman and Tom Marzolf collections.*

The bar at Wyandot. *Columbus Memory, Scripps-Howard Newspapers/Grandview Heights Public Library/photo.org Collection.*

Golf in Columbus at Wyandot Country Club

The guys enjoying the grillroom. *Betty Huber collection.*

much younger opponents off the tee, he invariably turns to them, smiles and facetiously remarks, "Great drive!" Dwight has nothing but fond recollections of Wyandot. "It was a special place," he says, "full of beauty and loads of golfing challenge."

When the members finished their appointed rounds, they found other diversions at the club. With Prohibition ending in 1933, the bar officially opened for the first time. And to paraphrase Claude Rains's character in *Casablanca*, you are probably not "shocked to learn that gambling was going on" at Wyandot. Ellen Marzolf Hallerman recalls two slot machines across from the bar. Ellen still remembers the time her father, Francis, gave her and her brother Frank nickels to try their luck.

Sometimes, higher stakes were played for. Legend has it that a lucky member won enough cash shooting craps one night at the club that his haul enabled him to buy a new sedan! With further improvements to the facilities, the club also became a hot spot for fraternity and sorority functions and dances when those organizations were looking for an off-campus venue to hold events.

Yes, Wyandot was a hoppin' place in the '30s. With the country still emerging from the Depression, country clubs had to tighten their belts, and Wyandot was no exception. But the members did not let enforced frugality stand in the way of a good time. Despite the gathering of storm clouds in Europe, most folks stateside retained an optimistic view of the future. And while Wyandot might not have possessed quite the social standing of Scioto or Columbus, it definitely had its own charm. Wyandot was the fun place to be!

Chapter 15

THE PRO'S PRO

His conservative, understated golf slacks were pressed with a sharp crease. His wavy hair, carefully parted down the middle, never had a follicle out of place. His strong, prominent chin and ramrod straight bearing projected inner strength and self-confidence. His professional career featured an array of accomplishments, including club making and designing, a notable swing aid invention, service to his local PGA section and an enviable playing record. More importantly, Elks/Wyandot pro Francis Marzolf was a principal member of a remarkably enduring golf family who has made major contributions to the sport for four generations. Almost from the inception of the game in America until the present day, the Marzolf family has been prominently employed in various facets of the game.

Edward Marzolf, Francis's father, hailed from the Alsace-Lorraine region bordering France and Germany. Edward's family was prominent in winemaking. In fact, the Marzolf vineyard produces fine champagne and other vintages to this day. But Edward determined that there might be a better life available in America, and he immigrated to the United States through Ellis Island in the early 1900s. Edward found employment in Buffalo as the greenkeeper at the Country Club of Buffalo. The quality of the course was such that the USGA selected it to host the 1912 U.S. Open. Francis, then eight years old, had the opportunity to study great players up close, including winner Johnny McDermott, Jim Barnes and Walter Travis. Francis was clearly destined to have a career in golf. Virtually all of the Marzolfs derived their living from the game. Two of Francis's brothers,

Francis Marzolf. *Ellen Marzolf Hallerman and Tom Marzolf collections.*

Ray and Martin, followed their father into greenkeeping. Gene, a third brother, sold golf maintenance equipment for Toro in California. His sister, Bernadean, would marry prominent Ohio golf professional Charlie Lorms.

But Francis was easily the best player in the family, and in 1922, Lorms consequently hired his nineteen-year-old brother-in-law to serve as his assistant at the posh Columbus Country Club. The young man invariably showed up for work nattily attired in a starched shirt and tie on even the hottest summer days. He didn't just give lessons and compute handicaps. Francis moonlighted

The Wyandot Years, 1931-46

Young Francis Marzolf in his days as an assistant to Charlie Lorms at Columbus Country Club. *Ellen Marzolf Hallerman and Tom Marzolf collections.*

designing and handcrafting clubs for the Burke Golf Company. Burke Golf, located in nearby Newark, Ohio, was a leading manufacturer of golf clubs during that era. Burke hickory-shafted clubs stamped with Francis's initials are among the Marzolf family's most prized possessions.

Francis and Charlie became the closest of friends and confidants. The older Lorms, with loads of club pro experience at Oakland Hills and Inverness, was an ideal mentor for the young apprentice learning his trade. Charlie and his wife also played a key role in Francis's personal life. The Lorms introduced Francis to Mary Dehner, and the young couple married in 1926. After serving four years under Charlie's tutelage at Columbus, Marzolf accepted the head professional position with Arlington Country Club. He remained at Arlington for four years, steadily building his reputation as a preeminent instructor. Though only twenty-six, Francis Marzolf was already an accomplished seasoned pro when he left Arlington and succeeded Hermon Shute at The Elks in 1930. While it was definitely an upward move, Francis still had to scuffle some to make ends meet. So to pick up extra money during the winter, he gave indoor golf lessons at downtown Columbus's Neil House Hotel.

Golf in Columbus at Wyandot Country Club

A club pro's job is generally a dawn-to-dusk affair with little time left over to hone the game that attracted him into the profession in the first place. Nevertheless, Francis Marzolf played some excellent competitive golf. He was most proud of qualifying along with Charlie for the 1928 U.S. Open. He qualified a second time in 1933. His rousing 64, carded at Wyandot in the late '30s, was second only to Denny Shute's 1928 course-record 62. Whenever a big-name pro came to town to play an exhibition match, Francis was on the short list to fill out a four-ball. He always gave a good account of himself in these affairs, battling great players like Walter Hagen, Craig Wood and Joe Kirkwood on even terms. Later in his career, he won the Teacher's Trophy for the Southern Ohio Section of the PGA in both 1954 and 1955, earning him berths in the national PGA Seniors Championship held in Dunedin, Florida. He underscored his senior success in 1955 with a victory in the Southern Ohio Seniors Championship.

But it was as a golf instructor that Francis achieved his greatest distinction. He stressed adherence to the fundamentals with his students: a good grip, proper alignment and keeping a steady head position throughout the swing. Having observed that, despite his best advice, many pupils were unable to prevent their heads from bobbing up and down or from side to side during the swing, Francis conceived of a device to stop this flaw. It became known as the "Marzolf Machine." *Golfdom* magazine published a feature story describing how this rather cumbersome but effective swing aid functioned.

> *The device consists of a 7 ft. pipe arising from a heavy iron base. Horizontally from that pipe extends another pipe at the end of which is a leather skullcap, attached to the pipe by a roller-bearing pivot. The golfer takes his correct stance, the cap is fitted by raising or lowering the arm, and the stage is set for practice.*

The machine received rave reviews when Francis demonstrated it at Purdue University. He applied for a patent and was prepared to market the device nationally before World War II intervened.

Francis's greatest achievement as a teacher was making Mrs. Thornton Emmons into a state champion golfer inside of five years after she took up the game. Glen Bishop, Wyandot's 1930 Ohio Amateur winner, credited Marzolf with helping him transform his occasionally erratic play into championship form. Many other prominent players, including Ohio native and future PGA champion Dow Finsterwald, benefitted from Francis's keen eye and sage advice. Joanie Terango, still a fine player at her home club of Brookside, took lessons from Francis at age eight in the late '40s. Her

The Wyandot Years, 1931-46

The Marzolf Machine. *Ellen Marzolf Hallerman and Tom Marzolf collections.*

memory of Francis is still fresh in her mind: "I remember Francis Marzolf as being big and handsome. My sister and I were so excited to take lessons from him because we had heard he was a really special local player. I was so lucky to have the advantage of his expertise at an early age. I guess that's one of the reasons I love the game so much."

While employed at Wyandot, Francis also continued his involvement in club making as a staff member with MacGregor Golf. MacGregor manufactured a line of irons designed by Francis with the Marzolf signature emblazoned thereon.

GOLF IN COLUMBUS AT WYANDOT COUNTRY CLUB

Francis's twelve years at The Elks/Wyandot were happy ones. Naturally genial, he enjoyed excellent relations with club members. Francis was kind and helpful to everyone at Wyandot, but he was not perceived as playing favorites—a common tripwire for sociable pros. His wife, Mary, helping out with sales activities in the pro shop, was likewise a whiz in the social skills department.

Francis probably never would have left Wyandot but for the war. As a result of the hostilities, he took leave from the club in 1942 and provided governmental service as a property manager for the Defense Homes Corporation. In 1945, he returned to golf by taking on the dual role of golf professional and general manager of York Temple Country Club, just north of Wyandot. Francis was well respected by his peers and was chosen to serve in various capacities with his local PGA section, including the section's president. In 1958, Marzolf was voted the Golf Professional of the Year for the Southern Ohio Section. After thirteen years at York, Marzolf was hired as the professional at Brown's Run Country Club in Middletown, Ohio, where he finished his career. Shortly after retiring in 1969, sixty-five-year-old Marzolf suffered a massive, fatal cerebral hemorrhage. He was stricken just after mailing a box of Mary's cookies to son Frank's family.

Francis was far from the last of the Marzolf family to make significant contributions to golf. His nephew Johnny Lorms, the son of Francis's sister Bernadean and Charlie Lorms, led the Ohio State Buckeyes to the NCAA championship in 1945. Johnny also took down the NCAA individual title that year. His classic swing was visible at an early age.

Francis's daughter, Ellen Marzolf Hallerman, also achieved golfing success at Ohio State. Despite being surrounded by a golfing family, Ellen had shown little interest in the game until she came to the university. But after taking a golf class from OSU instructor and former Wyandot star Blanche Sohl, Ellen discovered she had an aptitude for the game. She improved so quickly that she gained a spot on the women's team's starting lineup. The team caught fire and won the National Collegiate Golf Tournament for Women in 1947—a feat still commemorated on a plaque at the OSU Golf Course. Ellen lettered four years (1947–50) on the women's team. Further Marzolf family involvement in golf came about when Ellen's brother Frank Marzolf (himself a four-year starter on the University of Notre Dame's golf team from 1949 to 1952) married Ellen's OSU teammate Rita Favret.

Frank Marzolf's son, Tom Marzolf, represents the family's fourth generation in the game. Based on his remarkable body of work with Fazio Golf Course Designers Inc., Tom is regarded as one of America's finest golf course architects. He is particularly renowned

The Wyandot Years, 1931–46

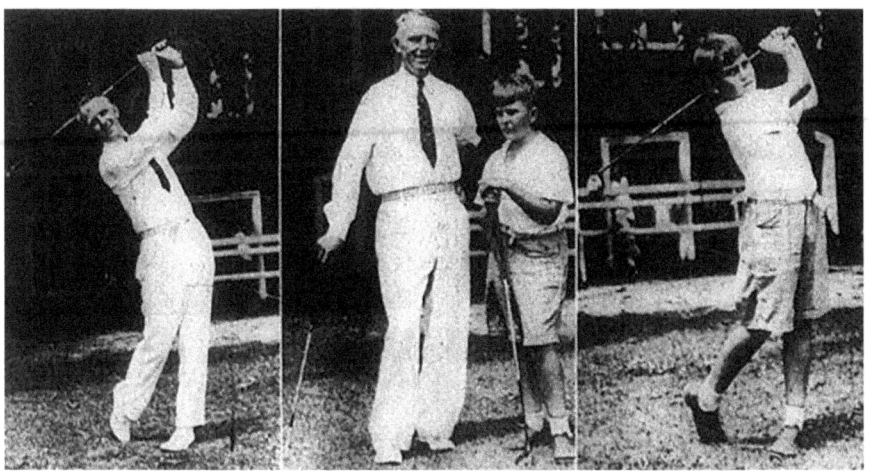

Above: Charlie Lorms, brother-in-law and mentor to Francis Marzolf, with son Johnny Lorms, who became the NCAA champion in 1945. *From the* Columbus Citizen, *August 4, 1936.*

Right: Rita Favret and Ellen Marzolf Hallerman. *Ellen Marzolf Hallerman and Tom Marzolf collections.*

for his remodeling of classic courses to get them major championship-ready. His refurbishment of Merion Golf Club in preparation for the 2013 U.S. Open was universally praised. He is currently working as the design consultant for Oakmont Country Club to assist with

Tom Marzolf and daughter Clara. *Courtesy of Tom Marzolf.*

preparing that club's epic course for the 2016 U.S. Open. Tom is a past president of the American Society of Golf Course Architects.

Will there be another golfing Marzolf representing the family's fifth generation in the game? Perhaps so. Tom Marzolf reports that daughter Clara has attended the Pinehurst Golf Camp, possesses an excellent swing and is working diligently on her game.

The extended Marzolf family has been engaged in virtually every aspect of the game: golf course architecture, superintendence of courses, equipment sales, administration, club management, club making and serving as golf professionals. Francis's contributions to that golf legacy were profound. He inspired succeeding generations of Marzolfs to follow him into the game. To those who knew him at The Elks/Wyandot and other clubs he served, he was the best of men, respected and liked by all. In short, Francis Marzolf was the consummate pro's pro!

Chapter 16
VICTORY GARDENS

As the 1930s gave way to the '40s, things seemed to be going reasonably well at Wyandot. With the Great Depression having finally run its course, the country's improved economic outlook boded well for the club's fortunes. Despite the economic turmoil of the past decade, Wyandot had successfully established itself as a mid-priced, no-frills golf club with an outstanding course and a stable of excellent low-handicap players, both male and female. But a potential threat to Wyandot's continued existence always loomed, given that the club was merely a tenant in a series of short-term leases with its landlord, Glen Burn.

With club patron John W. Kaufman gone, Wyandot was dependent on the continued benevolence of the remaining Glen Burn partners, including Harold Kaufman, Oscar "Dutch" Altmaier and perhaps other beneficiaries of the John Kaufman estate. Harold enjoyed a long history with the club, having chaired the construction committee that built the Donald Ross–designed golf course. He remained active in the club, still serving on its board of directors. Harold probably would have been satisfied with continuing the "nominal" rent originally arranged by his father with the club in 1931. But it is unlikely that his partners enjoyed the same level of allegiance to Wyandot. One or more of those partners must have grown frustrated with the paltry revenue generated from their tenant, and Harold might have been under pressure to remedy the situation. Even before the war, Harold Kaufman was urging club members to buy the property from Glen Burn. Dwight Watkins tells this story: "My father, Cy, was a Wyandot member in those days. He told me that Kaufman approached the members several times, saying, 'You fellows have to buy it or else we'll have to sell to someone else!' No one believed him because Mr. Kaufman already had plenty of money."

However, the financial difficulties of clubs like Wyandot soon seemed trivial once the country plunged into war on December 7, 1941. Far more than any other war this country has fought, World War II received unqualified popular support. Most agreed that all activities on the home front must take a backseat to the goal of obtaining victory. While the advent of the war presented hardships for all leisure-related activities, golf clubs and courses encountered the greatest challenges by far. They were broadsided from every direction. In retrospect, it is a wonder that most of them survived the war.

The hits to the business of golf were pervasive and far-reaching. The first was the Office of Price Administration's (OPA) edict ordering the rationing of automobile tires in January 1942. This measure was designed to discourage motorists from pleasure-driving to places like golf courses. Then, in May 1942, the OPA ordered the discontinuation of golf ball manufacture for the duration of the hostilities. But the hardships caused by those measures paled in comparison to those caused by the imposition of nationwide mandatory gas rationing, effective December 1, 1942. Most motorists were limited to the purchase of three gallons of gasoline per week. This mandate presented an enormous dilemma for all clubs and courses. With such a severe gas consumption limitation, how could golfers get to their respective courses—particularly those more remote "country" clubs located several miles from the centers of population?

Wyandot did its best to address gas rationing. The club formed a transportation committee to figure out how to get its golfers to the course with "a minimum of gas and rubber consumption." The *Columbus Evening Dispatch* noted that the committee was engaged in working out the details of a "share the ride" program, "but if this should prove inadequate, the committee might resort to horse-drawn vehicles, or a station wagon from the High Street car line to the course." Rationing also caused a predictable reduction in dining and other use of Wyandot's facilities. The *Dispatch* noted that "dinners will be discontinued to be replaced by light luncheon service."

Even assuming a golfer expended his precious rationing coupons to reach the course, who was going to carry his clubs? Golf carts would not come into general use until 1951. The supply of professional caddies had dwindled down to a handful, as most had entered the service or related essential industries. The concept of carrying one's own clubs was an alien one to most club members—a point well-made by Byron Nelson, then the professional at

The Wyandot Years, 1931-46

Toledo's Inverness Club. "Lord Byron" offered the view that "country club golfers simply won't play if they have to carry their own sticks."

It took a while for the effects of the draft to be fully felt by Wyandot, but by the spring of 1943, most of the male members age thirty-eight and younger were either in military service or engaged in essential industries. Paul McNutt of the War Manpower Commission affirmed in February 1943 that "by the end of this year 10 out of 14 of the able-bodied men between 18 and 38 will be in the armed services." Another blow was struck that month when McNutt issued an order effective April 1, 1943, listing the various job occupations that would be classified as "non-essential." Those men so engaged were required to find "essential" work or be drafted. Among the positions considered nonessential was that of a greenkeeper. Thus, most courses were depleted of their crew members unless they were over the maximum draft age. Wyandot's greenkeeper, Lawrence Huber, was already fifty-two years old and well beyond draft eligibility. Still, as aforementioned, he harbored a patriotic urge to serve his country, so in the spring of 1943, Huber left Wyandot and accepted a position maintaining military airfields for the U.S. Army Corps of Engineers.

Wyandot's professional of twelve years, Francis Marzolf, also left the club, taking a position managing military housing units in Columbus. The club, saving expenses wherever possible, decided not to replace him for the time being, electing to get by solely with a sales person in the pro shop.

With the loss of membership causing a corresponding loss of revenue (most clubs estimated that gross revenues were down 50 percent), Wyandot could afford only the barest of skeleton crews. Thus, a "share the work" program was instituted, wherein the remaining members would run the club themselves. Ten committees were established to "plan the 1943 season, meet all of the emergencies, and maintain golf and golf facilities."

Some sports could afford to place their facilities in mothballs and await a successful conclusion to the war. Russ Needham of the *Dispatch* wrote frequently on this subject and made the point that the decision to discontinue golf course maintenance meant the loss of the course:

> *There won't be a golf course as such, there anymore. It'll just be pasture, fit for growing corn and potatoes perhaps, but you can't putt on pasture, and you can't blast out of a bramble bush...If they* [the golf clubs] *let their course go unkempt for a season, or even a month or so, at the critical time of year, the greens will be gone beyond all redemption...Replacing a green of average size would cost in the neighborhood of $1,000. That's one green,*

> *and there are 18 on a golf course…So, the problem of the golf clubs is, shall they suspend, as most sports could if necessary? If they do, it means an expense of upward of $25,000 to rebuild them in that glorious day after victory. Or do they keep them up as best they can, gambling the expense now will be less than to rebuild later. And if they decide on this, who'll do the work and who'll pay for it?*

This was a dilemma faced by even the most prestigious clubs. Augusta National dealt with the issue in part by allowing a herd of cattle to roam the course in hopes that the cows' grass munching would stay ahead of the growth of the turf.

Wyandot did its best to keep the course playable and opened the course for the spring season on April 2, 1943. Most of the other clubs managed to follow suit. Brookside, refuting rumors that the club would not operate in 1943, opened as well. However, Dublin-Arlington, Columbus's oldest course, did close down. The Columbus District Golf Association announced that it was canceling its tournament schedule for the season. The CDGA, struggling to keep tournament golf alive in some fashion, stated that it would consider sponsoring and running war relief events "which might be suggested by and co-sponsored by the USGA and other agencies."

Once on the course, club golfers faced further obstacles that were arguably more oppressive than all the others: guilt and derision. Golfers were often made to feel unpatriotic by indulging in a rich man's pastime while U.S. soldiers were fighting and dying overseas. "Don't you know there's a war going on?!" was a common refrain heard by those engaged in recreational pursuits, especially golfers.

The *Dispatch*'s Russ Needham, in a column sympathetic to stigmatized golfers, referenced one of Wyandot's players to illustrate the club player's plight:

> *Bill Margraf, whose rich locker-room baritone should not be lost in the turmoil, come what may, is a little dismayed at the prospect of what the summer will bring…Bill feels a little timid about taking his spoon or mashie in hand…Bill flinches to think how he'll feel if, as he tees off No. 4, which is near the highway, some blighter will be coming down Morse Rd. on very vital business of course, and shouts "slacker" into his sensitive ears.*

That stigma reached high into the ranks of the professional golfers as well. The PGA suspended most tournament operations in 1943, conducting only three events. Most of the pros were in service or working for essential

The Wyandot Years, 1931–46

industries for the duration of the war. Denny Shute came back to Columbus and performed his service working as an inspector for Jeffrey Manufacturing.

Denny and his wife settled down in a farmhouse with ten acres located on Hard Road on the northwest side of Columbus. When not engaged with Jeffrey, Shute busied himself with chores.

Shute still managed a weekly game in the Columbus Golf League as the ace player on the KingTaste team. During wartime, the league permitted each team to have one professional. Imagine having to go head to head with a three-time major champion without benefit of strokes!

Wyandot and the other clubs searched for ways to maximize revenue while still contributing to the war effort. The club instituted the category of "governmental memberships." This was viewed by the *Dispatch* as a "combination of thoughtful hospitality and a desire for self-preservation." Such memberships were reserved for males "not resident but temporarily located in Franklin County." The new membership

Denny Shute at his Hard Road farm. *From the Columbus Evening Dispatch, May 31, 1942.*

category was designed to garner new members from essential industry employees and men in the armed services. The dues for this new category were set at ten dollars per month with no initiation fees. Wyandot's president, Paul Anderson, was cautiously optimistic, stating that "our membership drive is exceeding expectations." York Temple adopted a ten-dollar membership fee with the proviso that the member would have to pay a thirty-cent greens fee for each round played.

Golf in Columbus at Wyandot Country Club

Halfway through the summer of '43, the clubs and the CDGA began to find ways to contribute to war relief through tournament competition. All of the clubs in the Columbus district sponsored "Hale America" golf events over the Fourth of July weekend to benefit the Red Cross. On July 18, the CDGA saw fit to hold its first competition of the season—a mixed two-ball foursome event at Columbus with all entry fees likewise being donated to the Red Cross.

Another means by which the clubs contributed to the war effort were the numerous victory gardens planted in their spare space. The gardens were used to plant vegetables, fruit and herbs with the intent of reducing pressure on the public food supply. Maintenance of these gardens also helped boost the morale of those tending them. Every private club in the Columbus district established a victory garden, and this produced a spirit of friendly competition to determine which club's garden was the best. Columbus and Scioto plowed and planted four acres. Wyandot reserved plots for sixty members over five acres. Brookside boasted the largest garden, with seven acres cultivated. That club even hired a man to "pitch a tent on the course and do night patrol duty in the 'victory garden' areas."

Bob Kepler stakes out a victory garden. *From the* Columbus Evening Dispatch, *April 4, 1943*.

The Wyandot Years, 1931-46

Despite these burdens, there was still some stellar golf played by Wyandot members during the war years. The men's club team won the season-long interclub competition in 1941. Johnny Florio, now thirty-five, shot a 64 at his home course on July 4, 1944, tying Francis Marzolf for the second-lowest tally scored at Wyandot. Two other notable amateurs—Ray Heischman and Byron Jilek—joined the club for brief periods. Jilek, an amazingly consistent ball striker, was a particular standout. From 1933 to 1936, he played for Miami University's golf team, serving as captain his senior year. Before moving to Columbus, he won Zanesville Country Club's championship. He was good enough to match up in exhibitions with the likes of Byron Nelson and Chick Evans. Upon moving to Columbus in 1942, he joined Wyandot and made a run at winning the District Amateur that year before bowing out in the semifinals. But Jilek did not stay long at Wyandot, moving over to York Temple in 1944. His exodus might have been the result of constant rumors that the course's grounds were about to be sold to the State of Ohio. Jilek enjoyed a distinguished career in local golf circles, winning the first of his three District Amateur titles in 1947. He ultimately left York Temple for Brookside, where he became a many-time club champion.

Unfortunately, there was a factual basis underlying the ongoing gossip surrounding the club's sale. Negotiations between Glen Burn and the State of Ohio were heating up. It is reasonable to assume that the financial hardships caused by the war had further compromised Wyandot's ability to make rental payments to Glen Burn. But was Glen Burn motivated to sell because it wanted to rid itself of an investment that was not working out, or was it because the state (as intimated in a Russ Needham column in the *Dispatch*) was threatening to initiate condemnation proceedings anyway, and that partnership resistance to governmental acquisition would be futile? Or both? Given the prior repeated efforts of Harold Kaufman to divest the property to the club's members, both rationales are plausible.

In July 1944, Glen Burn sold the entire property to the State of Ohio for $100,000. The state desired to replace the existing Hogwarts-like Ohio School for the Deaf located on Town Street in downtown Columbus with an up-to-date facility.

The state was also seeking land for the Ohio School for the Blind, then located on Parsons Avenue in Columbus. The Wyandot property would allow each school to maintain its own separate campus on either side of the ravine.

As the transaction with the state loomed, Russ Needham lamented the anticipated passing from the scene of the wonderful Wyandot course. But it wasn't the only golf property on the chopping block. It appeared that

Golf in Columbus at Wyandot Country Club

Ohio School for the Deaf in downtown Columbus. *Columbus Memory, Scripps-Howard Newspapers/Grandview Heights Public Library/photo.org Collection.*

Indian Springs and Brookside were also soon to be sold. The latter course had become the target location for the new state fairgrounds. Needham commented that Brookside's remote location "in these transportation-ridden days is unfortunate. Its chief assets are a fine and enthusiastic membership and a delightful clubhouse, although the golf course itself is inclined to be on the monotonous side. It might be, in some distant day, the members of Wyandot and Brookside, backed by the funds they will receive for their clubs, will see fit to get together, buy land in some new location and restore the best features of each club into one sterling organization." (Brookside was never acquired by the state, and it survives to this day as one of the city's finest courses).

But Needham was clearly saddest about what appeared to be the imminent closing of Wyandot. Waxing eloquently, he described the beloved track this way: "It wasn't long and it wasn't difficult, as long as you kept it straight. But it was a delight to play. It was like a cool soothing hand on a fevered brow on a hot day. It had calmness and dignity combined with a suggestion of the joy of living. There were few golf courses like it. It's a shame it has to go."

But despite the sale, the story of The Elks/Wyandot was not at an end. There would be several more episodes in the course's narrative.

PART III

The Municipal Course Years,
1946–52

Chapter 17
REPRIEVE!

It must have been a bittersweet feeling to have been a member of Wyandot Country Club in the summer of 1946. On the positive side of things, the war was over. With rationing and self-sacrifice now behind them, the club's golfers could play their rounds guilt free. All of the area courses were bustling with activity. And despite the sale of the course property to the State of Ohio, golf was still being played at Wyandot. The press of other postwar spending priorities had, for the time being, stalled the state's plans to construct new schools for the blind and deaf. The state had decided to let the country club continue occupancy under short-term lease arrangements until it was ready to proceed with construction.

But the members realized this reprieve was only temporary and that it was only a matter of time before their course would be lost. With memberships beginning to fill up at Brookside, York Temple, Columbus and Scioto, many Wyandot members worried that if they procrastinated in switching to one of the other golf clubs, they might have trouble gaining membership or be forced to mark time on a waiting list. Thus, a steady stream of member resignations began to hit the club manager's desk. There was little reason to be the last man or woman out the door.

Still, a hardy band of surviving members did their best to hold things together in 1946. The club even hired a new man to fill the golf professional slot that had been vacant since Francis Marzolf left in 1942. The new pro, mustachioed Al Marchi, could really golf his ball. He won a wide assortment of local professional events and subsequently became the Ohio Open

Spectators' view from behind the par-three fifth hole at the 1948 Columbus Invitational. *Columbus Memory, Scripps-Howard Newspapers/Grandview Heights Public Library/photo.org Collection.*

Champion in 1947. He was a good enough player to take a brief flier on the pro tour. Buoyed by the sponsorship of Dayton diamond merchant Jack Werst (the owner of the Vanderbilt and Styx diamonds), Al competed in several tour events in the summer of 1950.

The Municipal Course Years, 1946-52

Marchi was a talented teacher of the game as well. A prized pupil was Ohio State golfer Bonnie Randolph, who later enjoyed a distinguished career on the LPGA tour, garnering a victory and recognition by *Golf Digest* as that tour's "Most Improved Player" of 1958.

Both the Columbus District Golf Association and the Franklin County Women's Golf Association scheduled their respective championships at Wyandot in 1946. Presumably, both associations were cognizant of the fact that '46 was likely to be the last year that the club would be in existence. Harold Todd defeated Hammy Hedges 2 and 1 in a tense thirty-six-hole final to claim the CDGA title. The final of the Franklin County Women's Amateur at Wyandot proved to be a fitting last hurrah for the club and two of its most accomplished female players. In a rematch of their 1945 final, Mrs. William Margraf (formerly Chester Skees) downed her great friend and rival Sally Elson 4 and 2 to repeat as champion. Mrs. Margraf's wonderful final round of 80 kept Miss Elson at bay.

Faced with an untenable situation, the club finally gave up the ghost and disbanded after the 1946 season. For a while, it appeared that the course would lie fallow until the schools were built. But a master politician, gifted with a driving will and a love of golf, stepped forward to provide the course a lifeline. James Rhodes, then mayor of Columbus and later four-time Ohio governor, supported and promoted golf in myriad ways throughout his political career. In the spring of 1947, he was unhappy with the state of the city's municipal golf operations. The city's lone muni golf course, Twin Rivers (located where the Twin Rivers U.S. Post Office is now situated), was short and relatively unchallenging. Worse yet, the city only leased the Twin Rivers course, and the owners of the property were readying to build a large plant on the site, which would result in a further shortening of the course and moving of greens. According to *Columbus Evening Dispatch* sportswriter Paul Hornung, Twin Rivers was being "threatened with eventual abandonment." While discussions were ongoing regarding the feasibility of the city buying land and building another municipal course, nothing had yet come of them. The city desperately needed another golfing facility. Rhodes came up with a plan: with the state giving no sign that the schools at the Wyandot property would be constructed anytime soon, why not have the city operate the Wyandot course in the meantime? With luck, Wyandot could bridge the gap until the new facility was on board (eventually, a new muni—Raymond Memorial—opened for play in 1953). And who knows, maybe the mayor could work some of his vaunted political magic to further extend the life of the course!

Golf in Columbus at Wyandot Country Club

The state drove a hard bargain. While the agreed-upon annual rental of $1,680 was not overly burdensome, another clause in the lease was troubling. The government insisted on a thirty-day "notice to evacuate" clause as a condition of its leasing the property to the city. It was going to be challenging for the city's Parks and Recreation Department to safely plan a golf season—tournaments, leagues, etc.—knowing that the course might be forced to shut down in mid-season. But the mayor plunged forward and accepted the terms. With a stroke of the pen, the state, at the behest of Mayor Rhodes, had granted the Wyandot course a second reprieve.

Thrilled with the opportunity to play a top-level country club course, Columbus's publinx players flocked to Wyandot in 1947; 11,944 rounds were purchased by daily fee players. In addition, the city sold 181 annual "memberships." The city's annual report boasted that "by this acquisition, our citizens had an opportunity to play on a golf course equal in quality to a private course, at rates within reach of all."

Undaunted by concerns that the state could precipitously shut down the course, Rhodes showcased his new toy (Wyandot) by promptly scheduling it to host the seventy-two-hole state public links championship in June. This was simple enough for Rhodes to arrange since one of the many "hats" he wore was chairman of the state public links association. Val Chiaverini from Toledo, a three-time state publinx champion, posted a fine 291 total to win the title.

Throughout the summer of '47, Columbus golfers availed themselves of their newfound chance to play Wyandot. The availability of junior memberships was a particular boon to young golfers, affording them an opportunity to play golf frequently yet cheaply. Bill Amick was one of the youths who took advantage of the city's junior program. Bill later became a prominent golf course architect in Florida. His course design motto is "I want to see golfers smiling when they leave the eighteenth green!" By his own modest admission, he "never had a real job—I just hung around golf courses. I still do." A good player who competed collegiately at Ohio Wesleyan, Amick noted that most of the municipal players had difficulty hitting Wyandot's tight fairways. He observed that most "would have been better off with an axe instead of a nine iron!" Some golfers obtained an even sweeter deal than the juniors. Dr. Fred Balthaser, longtime respected rules official for the Columbus District Golf Association, was among them. As an employee of the city's Park and Recreations Department in 1947, he played the course for free!

Mayor Rhodes, ever restless in seeking out ways to promote golf in general and Wyandot in particular, came up with a beauty for 1948. Columbus Country

The Municipal Course Years, 1946–52

Club had hosted a PGA tour stop in '46 and '47—the Columbus Invitational. Managed by the "Zooligans," an eponymously named group that used the event as an opportunity to raise money for the Columbus Zoo, the Invitational

Program from the 1948 Columbus Invitational (sometimes referred to as the "Zooligans' Invitational"). *Author's collection.*

was a big deal. With a $10,000 purse, the first two events had attracted big-name entrants like Hogan, Snead, Nelson and Demaret. Nelson had won the tournament in 1946, and beknickered South African Bobby Locke had carried off top honors in '47. Columbus Country Club declined to host the Invitational a third year, so the venue for the '48 event was up for grabs. Rhodes pounced! The '48 Columbus Invitational would be held at Wyandot. How did the opportunistic mayor pull this one off? Easy—he was also was the man in charge of the Zooligans. With distinguished Judge Wayne Fogle in place as tournament chairman, the Zooligans and the city made Wyandot ready for the Invitational's opening round to be played the second week of July.

Of the top twenty-two PGA tour money winners, thirteen entered the '48 invitational (sometimes referred to as the "Zooligans' Invitational"). But not even Jim Rhodes's smooth talking was enough to entice top stars Sam Snead, Ben Hogan, Jimmy Demaret, Lawson Little, Jim Ferrier and Lew Worsham into the field. Their absence was conspicuous because each had played in the Invitational when it had been held at Columbus. The lightness of the purse certainly had something to do with their decision not to play. The PGA had recently adopted a rule recommending a minimum tournament prize money floor of $15,000. However, the Zooligans, figuring that an increased purse would jeopardize the zoo's charitable take, kept the pot at $10,000. Still, the field was star studded. Lloyd Mangrum, second leading money winner and 1946 U.S. Open champion, would be on hand. So would Bobby Locke, the third man in the money rankings and the Invitational's defending champion. The pundits felt that Locke's straight and "controlled" driving would be perfect for Wyandot, which "penalizes the 'strayer.'"

Other competing players who had won or would win major championships included Dr. Cary Middlecoff, Ed Furgol, Bob Hamilton, Chick Harbert, Jim Turnesa, Hermon Keiser and Columbus's favorite son Denny Shute, now forty-three. Tour stalwarts Dutch Harrison, Skip Alexander, Fred Hawkins, Ky Lafoon, Freddy Haas, Ellsworth Vines, Johnny Bulla, Johnny Palmer and Clayton Heafner were also gunning for the Invitational's first prize of $2,000. Toledo amateur and Champion Sparkplug scion Frank Stranahan couldn't accept prize money, but he was one of the 103 who teed it up. Rounding out the field were local luminaries Francis Marzolf, Danny Carmichael, Bob Kepler, Barney Hunt, Mel Carpenter, Pete Sohl and Pete Dye from Urbana—better known much later as one of the greatest golf course designers of his generation.

The Columbus newspaper scribes, happily ensconced in their quarters on the clubhouse's terrace, filled their columns with speculation as to whether

The Municipal Course Years, 1946–52
★ WORLD OF GOLF ★

Lloyd Mangrum
Dallas, Texas
Tam O'Shanter Country Club
Niles, Ill.

Photo of Lloyd Mangrum from the 1948 Columbus Invitational program. *Author's collection.*

Bobby Locke. *Jim Huber collection.*

Press area for the '48 Invitational on the Wyandot clubhouse terrace. *Columbus Memory, Scripps-Howard Newspapers/Grandview Heights Public Library/photo.org Collection.*

the short 6,433-yard, par-seventy-one course would withstand the onslaughts of the world's best.

Local pro Joe Thomas estimated that the winning score would be anywhere from 272 to 276. Joe allowed that the score could go higher, as any appreciable amount of wind would cause the course to tighten up considerably. Francis Marzolf forecasted a tally of 270 would get it done. Scribe Russ Needham predicted the first hole could give the big boys fits: "The green looks very inviting, but it's built like an inverted saucer. A pitch that lights in the middle with sufficient backspin will be safe enough…But a shot on the far side is apt to trickle off, possibly into some of the 1,000 tons of sand recently sprinkled about the place."

Controversy enveloped the tournament as soon as the pros hit the course for their practice rounds. Most complained about the length of the fairway grass and the rough around the edges of the greens. Lloyd Mangrum was particularly piqued and was vocal in his criticism. Presumably, the organizers were concerned that the pros would embarrass the short Wyandot course with rounds in the low 60s and elected to defend

The Municipal Course Years, 1946–52

Jim Huber tending to Wyandot's eighth green at the '48 Invitational. *Jim Huber collection.*

the course with high rough. But the criticism hit home, and Judge Fogle ordered the mowers out in force prior to the first round. Another fly in the ointment surfaced when a columnist from the *Columbus Citizen*, a morning newspaper, groused that the sports editor from a competing paper had "appealed to everyone except the ghost of Hitler in his successful effort to keep the first-day pairing list, or any part of it, from appearing Thursday in a rival sheet owned by the same family."

As with any golf tournament, it takes a squadron of volunteers to run the tournament. In the '48 Invitational, several came from the greenkeeping staffs of the other Columbus courses. University contributed young Jim Huber, son of longtime Elks/Wyandot greenkeeper Lawrence Huber. Jim repaired ball marks and raked the traps on Wyandot's eighth hole.

After Thursday's practice round, Chick Harbert, who, according to *Citizen* sportswriter Kaye Kessler, looked "more like a fashion plate than America's most potent man with a driver," emceed the pro's clinic. In what was a harbinger of the skill he would exhibit during the tournament, Mangrum put on the best show. Kessler reported that in the process of his three-iron demonstration, Mangrum hit "three hooks, three slices, three straight down the middle, three low wind balls, three straight out, and three that looked like 9 iron shots." In the driving contest, Skip Alexander bested long-knocker Harbert with a blow of 330 yards.

Golf in Columbus at Wyandot Country Club

The sun was hot, and the course severely baked out once the game was on for keeps. According to Kessler, the course was playing "faster than a pool table." The tented refreshment stand did a brisk business. Emerging to take control of the tournament was young San Francisco pro George Schoux. His sizzling thirty-six-hole total of 130 put him four ahead of Skip Alexander and up five over tournament tough Lloyd Mangrum. His score could have

George Schoux practicing at Wyandot's first green. *Bill Amick collection.*

The Municipal Course Years, 1946–52

been one shot lower, but Schoux called a penalty shot himself in the second round on Wyandot's thirteenth green when his ball moved slightly after he addressed it. No one noticed the infraction but Schoux himself. Winner of only one tour title, Schoux was regarded as a player with a great swing and talent, but also as one who had become obsessively devoted to practice. Some thought his single-mindedness was holding him back from greater success.

But overshadowing Schoux as the top story of the second round was Johnny Bulla's incredible double eagle on the par-five, 457-yard fifteenth hole. Evidently aided by the baked conditions, Bulla, Sam Snead's old

Johnny Bulla, the "Double Eagle Man." *Jim Huber collection.*

running mate on tour, drove 330 yards and then holed out from there. Nonchalant about the shot, Johnny shrugged and said, "I just took my niblick, and holed one out. That's all!" He shot a 67 that should have been lower. Unfortunately, Johnny tanked in subsequent rounds. Kaye Kessler of the *Citizen* reported that Bulla missed five three-foot putts in his Sunday afternoon round. Purging his frustration with Cary Middlecoff, Bulla then "broke his putter over his knee and handed over [to Cary] the two pieces."

Sunday's concluding double round turned into a two-man dogfight between soft-spoken Schoux and the thirty-three-year-old Mangrum. With his trim mustache and steely countenance, Lloyd appeared every bit the hard-bitten riverboat gambler. He lived the part, too, as he relished engaging in some of the tour's biggest money games. A crowd of eight thousand looked on as the two players went at it toe to toe for thirty-six holes.

Mangrum, cast as the patient hunter pursuing a seemingly vulnerable and slightly skittish prey, carded a brilliant 65 in the morning round. Schoux responded well, shooting a fine 67, but still the lead was trimmed to three strokes. The underdog Schoux came over as the more gallery-friendly of the two, smiling effusively and making eye contact with the patrons. He was quickly adopted by the crowd as its favorite. But playing the heavy was the last thing that would bother Mangrum, a twice-wounded veteran who had stormed Normandy Beach on D-Day. Eventually, his relentlessness wore his younger opponent down. Mangrum caught Schoux on the eighth hole of

Action on the ninth tee at the '48 Invitational. *Jim Huber collection.*

The Municipal Course Years, 1946–52

the afternoon round (watched closely by the aforementioned Jim Huber), passed him on the ninth and took a two-stroke lead on the eleventh. Playing safe, steady golf from there, Mangrum finished with a 68 and a winning total of 268. Runner-up Schoux, slumping a little down the stretch, finished with a final-round 72, leaving him a single stroke in arrears. When asked whether the penalty he had called on himself on Saturday had cost him the tournament, Schoux ruefully remarked, "It wasn't that stroke but a lot of others in that afternoon round Sunday," that did him in. "I tried," he shrugged, "and you can't do anything more than that."

Mangrum, sometimes brusque in his comments, was positively chatty at the trophy presentation. "I enjoyed this probably more than any other pro here, and I want to congratulate them for taking so many strokes."

The event was deemed a success. A beaming Jim Rhodes remarked, "This turnout this weekend is proof that Columbus wants and likes its golf." However, it was clear from Rhodes's remarks that he intended to

Winner Lloyd Mangrum and runner-up George Schoux at the '48 Invitational. *From the* Columbus Citizen, *July 12, 1948.*

Golf in Columbus at Wyandot Country Club

shelve the Invitational and focus his and the Zooligans' efforts on bringing a major tournament to Columbus. The *Dispatch*'s Russ Needham revealed that it was a near certainty that the PGA tournament (then played at match play) would be coming to Columbus in 1950. He thought that Columbus Country Club would be afforded the right of first refusal to host the event. Needham opined, "In the event of a refusal [by Columbus Country Club], Brookside and Scioto probably would be given the nod in that order." (The third choice—Scioto—was ultimately selected to host the '50 PGA.)

Rhodes also had to be pleased with the uniformly favorable reviews (aside from the pre-tournament long rough) of his municipal golf course. The tournament had provided a vehicle for Columbus golfers and followers of the sport to rediscover the beautiful Wyandot course. While the Columbus golf community had previously become reconciled to the fact that Wyandot would soon be closed, this question began to be asked again in 1948: "Why does this beautiful, historic golf treasure have to go?" Mayor Rhodes, playing his political cards with customary adroitness, certainly encouraged the growing drumbeat to somehow reverse the seeming inevitability of the course's closing. As 1949 dawned, the seeds sown by Rhodes to save the course began to bear fruit.

Scene from the 1948 Columbus Invitational with the clubhouse in the background. *Jim Huber collection.*

The Municipal Course Years, 1946–52

1948 Columbus Invitational Final Results

Player	Score
Lloyd Mangrum	268
George Schoux	269
Skip Alexander	271
Clayton Heafner	274
Bobby Locke	274
Dutch Harrison	276
Sam Byrd	276
Al Smith	276
Cary Middlecoff	277
Fred Haas Jr.	278
Ed Furgol	279
Ellsworth Vines	279
Frank Stranahan (am)	280
Johnny Palmer	280
Dick Metz	280
G. Webb	280
Marty Furgol	280

Chapter 18

SHOWDOWN!

On January 29, 1949, Mayor Rhodes authored a letter addressed to Dr. Thomas C. Holy, head of the Commission for New Residential Schools for the Blind and Deaf (the "Building Commission"). Rhodes urged Dr. Holy to take steps to have the Building Commission revisit its decision to locate the deaf and blind schools on the Wyandot course and consider building the facilities elsewhere. In making his pitch, the mayor extolled the virtues of Wyandot and its importance in meeting the needs of the city's municipal golfers. "This [Wyandot] is one of the finest golf courses in this section of the United States," Rhodes wrote. "It is vitally needed by the people of metropolitan Columbus as a municipal golf course. It has long been our dream that such a golf course might be added to our parks and playground system." Rhodes further extended an offer on behalf of the city to buy the Wyandot property from the state for $100,000—the same price the state had paid Glen Burn for the property in 1944. Realizing that his plea would have no chance of success unless a suitable alternative location for the schools could be expeditiously found, the mayor advised Dr. Holy that he would do whatever he could to help the Building Commission find a new site for the schools. Rhodes copied the state representatives from Franklin County with this letter. He was to later assert that he did so at the behest of attorney Dale Stump, counsel for the Ohio Federation of Organizations of the Deaf (OFOD). Stump's involvement was later to be the subject of controversy.

Holy responded that the Building Commission would be willing to "discuss a trade" of the Wyandot site. But since it was the Holy-led Building

The Municipal Course Years, 1946–52

Photo of Mayor James Rhodes from the 1948 Columbus Invitational program. *Author's collection.*

Commission that had initially picked the Wyandot site for the location of the schools five years previously, he and his fellow commission members were far from eager to restart the entire process. Moreover, Rhodes's $100,000 offer was probably perceived as a lowball one. Recent real estate appraisals had established the value of the property at $300,000 to $350,000. Furthermore, the Building Commission had already spent roughly $230,000 for site-specific engineering and architectural plans and drawings, which would be money down the drain if the Building Commission acquiesced to the mayor's request that the state jettison its plans to erect the school facilities on the Wyandot property.

Dr. Holy had done his best to exercise prudence regarding the $5.5 million budget appropriated by the legislature for building the schools. He had delayed the start of construction after receiving the plans in 1947, waiting patiently for exorbitantly high postwar construction costs to decline to the point where the entire project could be built without exceeding the budget. Now, with those costs finally receding some, he was anxious to get the project underway. Dr. Holy had to be frustrated with Rhodes's meddling. But it would not be good politics to blow off the popular mayor whose name was being bandied about as a potential Republican candidate for governor in the upcoming 1950 elections. So regardless of what his private thoughts might have been, Dr. Holy publicly expressed a willingness to entertain alternative sites for the schools.

As the savviest of politicians, Jim Rhodes no doubt realized that his leverage over the Building Commission was limited and that it would be difficult to cause it to reverse course by himself. To save Wyandot, officials from other branches of state government would need to apply pressure also. To the mayor's delight, a fellow Columbus Republican serving in the Ohio House of Representatives stepped forward to help Wyandot's cause. Representative Robert Shaw sponsored several legislative bills designed to torpedo efforts to build the schools at the Wyandot site. His first proposed measure, House Bill 528, recommended for passage by the House Judiciary Committee, would have authorized the state to sell the golf course property to the City of Columbus for $135,000. Shaw justified this by arguing that the state had paid $100,000 and invested an additional $35,000 (ignoring the much higher engineering and architectural expenses already incurred). In doing so, Shaw took pains to mention that he was not opposed to the construction of new buildings for the two schools. The "present blind and deaf schools could be razed and new buildings constructed on the present site or on other sites acquired." Representative Shaw parroted Rhodes's argument regarding the importance of the Wyandot golf course to the community. "There is plenty of land in Columbus and Franklin County for the schools without taking our best golf course," said the lawmaker.

Shaw also attempted to introduce an amendment to an appropriation bill that would have required the "new buildings to be constructed on the present location of the present blind and deaf schools." Dr. Holy was aghast at this gambit. He promised that his commission "would oppose as vigorously as possible" any such measure. Dr. Holy expressed the view that the schools' current locations were "too small. They are in congested areas where traffic is a hazard to the handicapped. Modern trends in treatment of the blind and the deaf stress broader programs of vocational and agricultural training. More space is required." Impressed with Dr. Holy's argument, the Finance Committee rejected Shaw's proposed amendment.

The Municipal Course Years, 1946-52

But Shaw's crusade to assist Rhodes and preserve the course was far from over. He then sought to persuade the House Finance Committee to recommend the re-appropriation of funds for school building construction on the condition that the facilities not be built on the Wyandot property. When the committee agreed to this condition, it seemed that the fight to save the course had finally succeeded. The *Citizen*'s June 23, 1949 headline declared that the golf course advocates had carried the day.

An "elated" Mayor Rhodes praised the committee's decision and indicated he would "redouble his efforts to find suitable sites for the schools." Rhodes announced that the city "will co-operate with the schools' Building Commission in every possible way." But the mayor was well aware that the Finance Committee's recommendation was not final and that the General Assembly could reject it. The likelihood of such a rejection would increase significantly if Rhodes could not quickly find a suitable alternative site for the schools.

The question of whether the Building Commission should be permitted to proceed with its plans to build the schools on the golf course became a hot topic in the newspapers. Tellingly, none of the articles or editorials praised the Finance Committee's recommendation that the Building Commission find a new site. Instead, they expressed alarm at the deplorable conditions of both schools and urged immediate action. A June 28, 1949 editorial in the *Ohio State Journal* labeled the existing schools as "old, dilapidated firetraps...with the threat of horrible disaster hanging over them." It was stated that "the State of Ohio cannot afford to let the matter drift...The Legislature ought to make every provision it can for getting the schools built as soon as possible."

The *Columbus Citizen* ran two articles on June 26 and June 27 highlighting the two schools' overcrowded conditions and fire hazards. Both articles graphically depicted the schools' Dickensian environment. The article pertaining to the School for the Deaf included a photograph of an ancient bathtub that forty-four boys were forced to use for their Saturday night baths. An inspection of the school's dormitories indicated that the distance between the beds ranged from only twelve to fifteen inches. Adding to the danger of fire was the building's lack of fire escapes.

The *Citizen* reporter who visited the School for the Blind listed numerous deficiencies rendering the facility antiquated and unsafe: "Metal rods bolted to inside walls to keep the outer limestone wall from toppling...The top three floors of the six-story structure condemned 15 years ago...Boilers in the heating plant which were discarded 25 years ago at the Ohio

Golf in Columbus at Wyandot Country Club

Excerpt from the June 27, 1949 *Columbus Citizen* article relative to conditions at the School for the Deaf.

Penitentiary...An air shaft running through the center of the building which serves as a potential draft for fire."

On Monday, June 27, the Building Commission passed a resolution that ratcheted up the political heat on all concerned. The resolution reaffirmed the commission's selection of Wyandot as its first choice for the schools' location. The resolution further indicated that if Wyandot was not available, then locations outside of Columbus would have to be considered. Dr. Holy placed the blame squarely at Rhodes's feet. The mayor had pledged to find new sites but had not produced any. Thus, said Holy, "it seems unlikely suitable sites can be located in the Columbus area." Holy disclosed that three other communities had submitted proposals to house the facilities.

In response to that salvo, Columbus's labor and civic leaders joined the fray on Tuesday, June 28. Al Vesy, executive secretary of the Columbus Federation of Labor, spoke out vigorously in favor of keeping the project

The Municipal Course Years, 1946-52

in Columbus, stating, "Labor leaders here definitely want the buildings for new schools preferably in Columbus…The two schools furnish 200 jobs for employees."

By threatening to move the schools outside Columbus, Dr. Holy had cleverly created a sticky problem for the mayor. Rhodes's bread-and-butter issue throughout his storied political career was job creation. Rhodes would have found it unacceptable to play a part in causing existing Columbus-based jobs to migrate elsewhere. Desperate to find sites for the schools that would avoid such a calamity, the mayor enlisted the help of Columbus Real Estate Board president George Tifft. In short order, Tifft found two potential properties in the northern section of Franklin County, but they were outside the city limits. A third site in the southwestern portion of the city was also a possibility. Tifft gave assurances that Columbus utility services could be supplied to all three sites and that a fifteen-person committee he had formed "would be called to scour the county" to unearth more locations.

At the end of June, Jim Rhodes made a compromise offer to Dr. Holy: the city would offer property it owned on Trabue Road (later to become the Raymond Memorial Golf Course) as the new site for the schools. City hall officials indicated that "it would be cheaper to buy Wyandot for $125,000 than it would be to develop the Trabue Road site into a suitable course."

But Holy derisively rejected the offer out of hand, declaring, "Wyandot is a perfect spot for the schools. It has everything. The commission has looked at many sites and the best we have found is Wyandot." Dr. Holy's newfound intransigence probably came about because local press coverage and political forces were now swinging in the direction he favored—building the schools at Wyandot.

Entities representing the interests of the deaf and blind had heretofore stayed mostly in the background. But on July 1, the OFOD weighed in full force in favor of building the schools at Wyandot. The OFOD's attorney, Dale Stump, became the primary spokesperson for the group. Stump was far from a shrinking violet, and once he became embroiled in the controversy, his actions and statements were pointedly confrontational. His first move was to write George Tifft and recommend that his committee would be better off seeking an appropriate site for a new municipal golf course rather than looking for a new site for the schools. Turning Rhodes's fiscal argument against him, Stump argued that the state could be ahead financially if it built a new course for the city and proceeded with its plans to build the schools at Wyandot. He reasoned, "The State could save money by spending $100,000 for developing a new golf course site for Columbus instead of turning over

Golf in Columbus at Wyandot Country Club

Wyandot and losing $237,000 the State has invested in developing Wyandot for schools."

Heartened by the OFDF's support, the Building Commission immediately threw the gauntlet down to the General Assembly and voted to proceed with plans to erect the schools at Wyandot, notwithstanding the Finance Commission's recommendation to the contrary. The *Citizen* remarked that the commission "apparently is ignoring the committee action by proceeding with its plans." The OFDF was now calling out Mayor Rhodes for trying to take advantage of the state. An OFDF spokesman warned, "There is a serious danger that the mayor of Columbus in his enthusiasm to get a golf course for a fraction of its real value will try to high-pressure the state into accepting an inferior site in exchange." In a meeting of the OFDF in Cleveland on July 4, the organization raised the acrimony to new heights by passing a resolution contending that "Rep. Robert R. Shaw is conniving with Mayor Rhodes to grab the site for golfers at the expense of handicapped children."

In an eleventh-hour maneuver, a delegation from Akron consisting of representatives from rubber companies and labor organizations approached Governor Frank Lausche on July 5, urging that the schools be located in Summit County. Representative L.C. Washburn indicated that Akron had "at least three sites believed suitable, including one belonging to the county, which would be offered gratis."

Paul Fessenden, executive secretary of the Akron CIO, made a strong pitch for the Akron site. He stated, "Akron is the geographical center of the largest concentration of deaf mutes in the country outside of Pittsburgh," and 1,385 of them were "employed there mostly in the rubber industry."

Though a golfer—and a very good one—Governor Lausche did not react to Akron's proposal enthusiastically. He responded, "I am not now in a position to subscribe to your request. I do know the deaf are going to fight for Wyandot. I can understand how they feel to have the site promised them for four years and their hopes blasted." He further expressed his preference to have the schools "centrally located in the state to be available to all handicapped persons."

A final showdown between Mayor Rhodes and the OFDF's Stump took place at city hall on Wednesday, July 6. Fittingly, the meeting was held at "high noon," and bitter accusations were exchanged between the two men. Rhodes indignantly claimed that it was Stump who originated the "idea to stop the state from building the new schools at the golf course," adding that "we [the city] never would have entered the controversy if it hadn't been at your [Stump's] insistence."

The Municipal Course Years, 1946-52

According to the *Citizen*, "Stump lashed back with a denial and told Mayor Rhodes that the State would build the schools at the site despite the mayor's attempt to keep the golf course for the city."

While full of recriminations toward Dale Stump personally, the mayor extended an olive branch to the handicapped persons who Stump represented. "The land belongs to the State and the State can stick a shovel in it and start building today if it wants. Both the blind and deaf can depend upon us for co-operation. Our first interest is for the welfare of the children," said the mayor. It was clear by this statement that Rhodes had decided to back down and that his long fight to save Wyandot was ending. He was being mentioned as a candidate for governor, and he certainly did not want to be campaigning against a charge that he favored golfers over the needs of the handicapped.

That same day (July 6), the Ohio House of Representatives, by a vote of ninety-nine to twenty-three, struck from the appropriation bill the condition that the schools could not be constructed at the Wyandot golf course. Representative Shaw was not on hand for the vote, as he was fishing in Canada. An editorial in the *Citizen* expressed the following view: "We're glad the House defeated the amendment to an appropriation bill that would have barred Wyandot as a site...Columbus needs the golf course all right, but so do the blind and deaf children of the state need new schools. Unless some just as satisfactory alternate site can be made immediately available, the State should not give up the one it already has."

An editorial in the *Ohio State Journal* agreed with the position taken by the *Citizen* but also took the opportunity to throw the embattled mayor a bone: "Mayor Rhodes is to be commended for making it clear to the Legislature that it was not the City's intention to take the site away from blind and deaf children unless those immediately concerned so desired."

Jim Rhodes had sought to save Wyandot with relatively weak cards to play. He had played the hand dealt with his usual acumen, but it was not really a surprise that the needs of the handicapped ultimately trumped those of the city's golfers.

While Rhodes's efforts to save Wyandot by legislative action had failed, he continued to promote golf. In addition to being the man who brought the three Columbus Invitationals to town, he was also the catalyst for convincing the PGA to hold its 1950 championship at Scioto. He did not stop there. Rhodes was a great supporter of caddy scholarships, and it was for that purpose that he personally organized an annual caddy tournament in Columbus. The festivities included a pro-am event loaded with celebrities and star players. The 1951 benefit event at Brookside featured the likes

GOLF IN COLUMBUS AT WYANDOT COUNTRY CLUB

Memorial Tournament at Muirfield Village. *From left to right*: Bob Hope, Tom Watson, President Ford and Jim Rhodes. *Columbus Memory, Scripps-Howard Newspapers/Grandview Heights Public Library/photo.org Collection.*

of Ed Sullivan, Perry Como, Dizzy Dean, Sam Snead, Jimmy Demaret, Lawson Little, Lloyd Mangrum, the glamorous golfing sisters Marlene and Alice Bauer and wrestler Chief Don Eagle. Approximately seven thousand spectators enjoyed the action.

Later, Rhodes, a low-handicap player in his own right, became a fixture at Jack Nicklaus's Memorial Tournament at Muirfield Village. Whether paired with President Ford, Bob Hope or other famed personages, the four-time governor always made the featured foursome of the day. He was awarded numerous accolades for his contributions to golf. In 1981, he received the American Society of Golf Course Architects' Donald Ross Award. Given his persistent (though unsuccessful) effort to save a classic Ross course, the honor seemed especially fitting.

Finally free of interference, the Building Commission started entertaining bids for construction of the schools at Wyandot. This was a time-consuming process. The state permitted the city to continue operations at the golf course until the close of the 1950 season. Knowing the end was near, the self-styled "Wyandot Old-Timers" got together for one last round at the old course in the late summer. It had to be a bittersweet reunion for the old gang.

At summer's end, construction crews moved in and began taking the course apart. According to an article in the *Citizen*, "they ripped up thousands of

THE MUNICIPAL COURSE YEARS, 1946–52

Wyandot Old-Timers' Club, 1950. *Judith Florio collection.*

feet of the intricate watering system, dug huge holes in the middle of several fairways, and tore the furnishings out of the clubhouse." The city's lease was formally cancelled in November 1950. It seemed certain that no more golf would be played at Wyandot. But this great Donald Ross–designed course, which had survived numerous threats to its existence, was not quite ready to say goodbye!

Chapter 19

FINAL SHOTS

Her summer routine rarely varied: out of the house, located in the south end of town, by midmorning; a mile walk to the bus stop, where she would board the northbound bus; a twenty-five-minute ride through downtown and up High Street—the city's primary north–south artery—to the Morse Road stop; and then another mile hike east on Morse Road to the golf course. As fourteen-year-old Shirley Aisel would stroll up the long, curving driveway to the clubhouse, she might pause for a moment to eye the daily fee golfers putting on the seventh green or executing their pitch shots to the par-five sixth hole.

Having finally arrived, Shirley would check in at the pro shop, where she would be greeted by affable John Buchanan, who had served as Wyandot's pro-manager since the city took over operating the course in '47. If she had an extra quarter, she would treat herself to a "brown cow" (ice cream with root beer) in the clubhouse before grabbing her golf bag and heading over to the practice area by the railroad tracks. The young junior would usually spend hours working on her game and shagging her own balls. The girl would sometimes share practice time with young Dick Rhyan, who later made a name for himself on the PGA tour. Shirley enjoyed the routine of practice but relished playing the course most of all. It was so beautiful with its wooded ravines and ponds! But those woods spelled trouble for off-line shots, and she learned early the virtues of straight hitting. Comfortable in her Wyandot golf cocoon, Shirley Aisel improved rapidly in the summers of '49 and '50. She was good enough to play on the boys' team at South High School. In her golf reverie, Shirley remained relatively oblivious to the political machinations then threatening her beloved course.

The Municipal Course Years, 1946–52

It had not been the teenager's idea to take up golf. Shirley was given a rather firm push in that direction by her father, Glenn "Doc" Aisel. Doc had visions of his daughter playing on the LPGA tour and insisted that she practice. Doc had come up the hard way. He was one of eleven children. In what was retrospectively a rather remarkable coincidence, Doc's father and brothers labored in the Marble Cliff Quarries, excavating stone for John Kaufman's company. Instead of working in the quarry, Doc took up caddying at Scioto. He would walk down the middle of the fairway with all four bags (they were smaller then), and the Scioto members would walk over to Doc to retrieve their clubs. Having later secured gainful employment as a tool and die maker, Doc found time to take up golf himself. He became a very good amateur, ultimately winning the club championship at Indian Springs. One of Doc's best golfing buddies was Al Marchi, who had briefly served as Wyandot's professional. Doc and Al would team up in pro-ams all over Ohio and nearby states. When Shirley was a preteen, she recalls that the dapper Marchi was a frequent visitor to the Aisel household.

Shirley Aisel (now Shirley Edler) preparing to tee off on Wyandot's par-three fifth hole, circa 1952. *Shirley Edler collection.*

During the 1949 season, John Buchanan, unlike Shirley Aisel, was well aware of Wyandot's impending closing. Presumably, he could have gone through the motions of collecting greens fees and spent most of his time looking for his next employment. Instead, he actively marketed the course,

Golf in Columbus at Wyandot Country Club

Al Marchi with a very young and dimpled Shirley Aisel. *Shirley Edler collection.*

The Municipal Course Years, 1946-52

and municipal golfers continued to show up in droves. Buchanan also scheduled Wyandot for seven competitive tournament events during the '49 season. The course held its last statewide championship in June 1950, when it hosted the Ohio Public Links championship. In that contest, twenty-two-year-old Daytonian Jack Zimmerman prevailed one-up over perennial contender Val Chiaverini in a rain-drenched final match.

With the receipt of the state's notice to the city demanding that it vacate the premises in November 1950, it seemed certain that no more golf would be played at Wyandot. But John Buchanan launched his own private battle to keep the course alive a little longer. During the winter of '50–51, Buchanan "consulted with the city administration, the State, and the exponents of the blind and deaf schools." It was the pro's assessment that the "schools won't be needing more than a fraction of the Wyandot acreage for the next couple of years. Why not leave the rest of the course just as it is until the land is needed?"

This argument certainly struck a chord with Mayor Rhodes and city recreation director Nick Barack. Twin Rivers was barely playable, and Raymond Memorial would not be ready for play until 1953. The city still needed a golf course to bridge the gap until Raymond was opened. After much negotiation, the schools finally relented and granted the city a two-year lease. To work around the state's construction work, it would be necessary to reroute several

John Buchanan, Wyandot's last professional. *From the 1948 Columbus Invitational program.*

Golf in Columbus at Wyandot Country Club

holes, eliminate others and create some new, shorter ones. It fell to Buchanan to figure out a workable redesign. Ultimately, he was forced to shorten the course from 6,433 yards to 5,775. The course's par would be reduced from seventy-one to sixty-eight. Gone was the course's iconic dogleg tenth hole that had bedeviled nearly all except for Denny Shute, who would neatly cut the dogleg with a high spoon over the trees. Five new greens and six new tees were constructed. Seeding of the new fairways and greens was delayed until late in the spring of '51 due to foul weather and a "labor shortage so severe that John threatened to do the work himself." Buchanan and his wife, Helen, "scraped together what they could to refurnish the clubhouse. They got a piece of furniture from one city building and another there, making whatever repairs were needed, and finally again had a passable locker room." Buchanan tried to put the best face on things, saying that the "new 32-36-68 par would be considerably tougher than was the old 36-35-71." And the course's signature hole—the picturesque par-three fifth—was still intact!

Even the shortening of the course did not dissuade Buchanan from showcasing Wyandot in 1951. In August, the course hosted the Columbus Public Links Championship, which was won by Barney Hunt. The former district champion defeated Bill Podolski in the final, 2 and 1. But the bastardized layout was not as attractive as the old course, and as a result, the city recorded only 8,428 greens fees for the year.

Despite public awareness that its closing appeared imminent, the course continued to serve as the training ground for aspiring and talented young players. One of them was Bill Muldoon, who became a junior member in a most extraordinary manner. On a lark, the fourteen-year-old entered a hole-in-one contest at Olentangy Driving Range on Dodridge Avenue in June 1952 and won it with a shot that settled ten inches from the hole. His prize was a golf glove and season pass to what was left of Wyandot. Young Muldoon seized on what he viewed as a golden opportunity to develop his game, playing and practicing at Wyandot all summer long. According to brother Sam, Bill, like Shirley Aisel, was busing daily to Wyandot. His journey to the course required three such rides each way. His golfing summer at Wyandot paid off. Muldoon became an exceptional junior player, winning the state junior and Jaycee titles two consecutive years. That second year he bested young Jackie Nicklaus by one shot in both tournaments. In a February 2012 article in *Golf World*, Kaye Kessler remarked that before Jack could really think about beating Bobby Jones's records, "he had to beat Bill Muldoon." Bill's distinguished amateur record included three scholastic championships and a stint as a three-year letterman on the golf team at Ohio State. Perceiving that he could not keep up

The Municipal Course Years, 1946-52

Jackie Nicklaus (left) and Bill Muldoon were great competitors in the junior events—Bill often won! *From the* Columbus Citizen, *June 19, 1953.*

with the likes of Jack long-term, Bill did not pursue a career in golf and instead became a successful dentist.

Shirley Aisel Edler is quite sure that she and her dad were the last group to play at Wyandot in the late fall of 1952. She recalls her sadness to see the course on its last legs, just a shadow of what it had once been. But if Shirley and Doc were the last ones to play there, a more appropriate pairing to close the course could not be found. Both were outstanding players, and Doc's father had been associated with John Kaufman. Shirley would win fifteen Scioto Country Club championships between the years 1969 and 1995. She would take home several state senior women's championship trophies. Mrs. Edler still competes with success on Scioto's golf team. The Elks/Wyandot course, labeled by the scribes decades earlier as the "Maker of Champions," had made its last one!

GOLF IN COLUMBUS AT WYANDOT COUNTRY CLUB

Shirley Edler still wakes up at night dreaming of old Wyandot. Instead of counting sheep, she tries to recall the holes of both the original course and John Buchanan's shortened redesign. Clearly, there was an unforgettable quality to the course that the construction of the two schools could not eradicate. Golfers still with us who had the pleasure of playing Wyandot—like Shirley, Dwight Watkins, Bill Amick, Kaye Kessler, Fred Balthaser and Sam Muldoon—would agree with the *Dispatch*'s Bill Needham's tribute. That esteemed sportswriter penned that the course was "a delight to play" and that it "had calmness and dignity combined with a suggestion of the joy of living. There were few courses like it."

Epilogue

By the mid-'50s, it was becoming difficult to discern that a golf course had once occupied the campus now occupied by the two schools. The School for the Deaf, located to the south of the ravine, fully covered the old clubhouse area. The School for the Blind, to the north of the ravine, removed any vestige of several holes on the back nine. Both schools remain in operation to this day.

In 1955, Harold Kaufman died at age sixty-five. Harold, who had succeeded his father, John, as the chief executive of Marble Cliff Quarries, had worked with Donald Ross on the course's construction committee at the time of its building in 1922 and hit the tee shot that opened the course in '23. Curiously, his obituary made no mention of his involvement with The Elks/Wyandot or his honorary lifetime membership in the BPOE.

Nor are there many remnants left of the Kaufman holdings. The Marble Cliff Quarry is now largely dotted with housing. Another of John Kaufman's companies, Claycraft Brick & Mining, closed up long ago. John W. Kaufman's plush Bryden Road home has been replaced by a nondescript apartment complex. The dire warning that the ancient School for the Deaf was a disaster waiting to happen finally came to fruition in 1981. A spectacular fire reduced much of the Neo-Gothic structure to ruins.

The remaining portion of the old school has recently been repurposed once more for use as a school. The Catholic Church–operated Christo Rey Columbus High School features a national educational program focusing on professional work-study programs for its students.

Epilogue

Aerial photo of the School for the Blind (top) and the School for the Deaf (bottom). *Columbus Memory, Scripps-Howard Newspapers/Grandview Heights Public Library/photo.org Collection.*

Epilogue

Christo Rey High School. *Courtesy of the author.*

Opposite, bottom: Fire at the old School for the Deaf, 1981. *Columbus Memory, Scripps-Howard Newspapers/Grandview Heights Public Library/photo.org Collection.*

The lodge homes of the BPOE have likewise disappeared. The building that served as the headquarters until 1915 has been replaced by the Columbus Commons parking garage. The Frank Packard–designed lodge home formerly located on Broad Street, for which John Kaufman served as chair of Lodge 37's building committee, has been long-since razed. The Midland Building is there today.

While many of the buildings and businesses of The Elks/Wyandot era have vanished, several of the folks who played the course are alive, very well and still playing excellent golf. On a crisp, sunny May morning, with the kind cooperation of officials from the Schools for the Deaf and Blind, I set up a date with three of them to visit the old course. All had made a distinctive mark in golf. Bill Amick, a Wyandot Country Club caddy who became a junior member once the course became municipally owned, visited from his home in Florida. Bill is past president of the American Society of Golf Course Architects and has spent his entire career designing and building golf courses. His entrée into

Epilogue

golf course architecture began when his boss on the greens crew at Ohio State, longtime Elks/Wyandot greenkeeper Lawrence Huber, recommended Bill for a graduate program in agronomy at Purdue University. The aforementioned Shirley Aisel Edler was on hand, too. Her fifteen club championship victories at Scioto have cemented her stature in the game. Rounding out the threesome that day was the irrepressible Dwight Watkins. Dwight's father, Cy, had been a member at Wyandot until the club disbanded. Dwight had caddied there and played the course many times. Both father and son became Brookside members in 1948. Dwight is the club's member of longest standing. He is a former club champion at Brookside.

They exuberantly scampered around the grounds with nearly the zest they would have exhibited over old Wyandot more than sixty years ago. Golf had certainly helped keep these three young! I thought it would be nice if they each hit a ceremonial shot. Employing a hickory-shafted niblick I supplied for the occasion, Bill, Dwight and Shirley all displayed timeless form in striking solid pitches to the general area of what had once been the sixth green.

Bill Amick, Shirley Edler and Dwight Watkins standing near the vista for the approach to what used to be Wyandot's third green. *Courtesy of the author.*

Epilogue

The Elks/Wyandot disappeared for good in 1952. While the Ross-designed golf course was certainly memorable, its greatest legacy is the golfing ambassadors and their progeny it produced. Amick, Edler and Watkins are great examples, but there were many more. Denny and Hermon Shute, Johnny and Judith Florio, Sam and Bill Muldoon, Glen Bishop, Lawrence and Jim Huber, Francis Marzolf, Ellen Marzolf Hallerman, Frank Marzolf, Glen Bishop, Mike Hurdzan Jr. and Sr., Bill and Chester Margraf, Dick Rhyan, Dick Gordin, Dr. Fred Balthaser, Al Marchi, John Buchanan, Sally Elson, Blanche Sohl, Mel Carpenter, Mrs. Thornton Emmons, Kaye Kessler, Byron Jilek, Ray Heischman, Herb Bash, James Reston Bob Kepler, Jim Rhodes, Lloyd Mangrum, Lloyd Gullickson and, of course, John and Harold Kaufman and Donald Ross all played significant roles on The Elks/Wyandot's stage and elsewhere in the golfing world. Their contributions continue to have a positive impact on golf and those they inspired.

Appendix

MEMORIES OF THE WYANDOT GOLF COURSE

By golf course architect William W. "Bill" Amick, ASGCA Fellow, Daytona Beach, Florida

My recollections of Wyandot go back to the 1940s. I often caddied there in 1946, which happened to be the country club's last season of operation. I was thirteen years old and had plenty of chances to get loops because at that time, golf carts and pull carts were not in use. If you played, you took a caddy or lugged your own clubs. After the city took over in 1947, I obtained a junior membership (for twenty dollars), which enabled me to play the course frequently. I have very clear memories of the course and how the holes looked and played.

I want to point out that playing equipment and the ability to maintain golf courses in the 1920s, 1930s and 1940s were much inferior to what we enjoy today. Golf balls did not fly as far, and clubs have since been vastly improved. Courses could not be so finely conditioned then. During dry spells, fairways got very hard on that ex-farmland. Drives and other shots could bound for a considerable distance. During soggy periods, especially in the spring, balls would plug in fairways or at best have little roll.

There was an adequate practice putting green and range. The range faced south, which was good regarding the sun. But the range was not as plush or used as much as practice areas are today at many courses. And in that era, there were no range balls available by the bucket. It was bring your own practice balls in a bag and have a caddy shag them for you. Most members seemed to head directly from their car to the clubhouse to the first tee to immediately start firing away, but I'm sure some of the better players used the practice facilities to perfect their games.

Wyandot had a variety of holes, which made it interesting to play again and again. It was certainly adequately challenging to all of its players. Some of its holes were laid out on mostly level land. The ravine with its slopes, eroded over centuries by a small creek, added contrast to the other holes. And there were potentially very punishing wooded areas next to many of the holes. Those mature trees could be highly troublesome for errant shots on holes in and on the sides of the ravine. The relatively shallow creek flowed to the west and roughly bisected where the course was located on the property. In one place, the creek had been dug out to create a pond on number five. Water hazards were not the critical strategic element of the course—it was trees and contours in a number of places. Those woods would often punish poorly planned or executed shots, particularly those of once- or twice-a-week players.

The course was not particularly long in total yardage even for its day, but some of its holes did require significant length, like numbers two, seven and thirteen. The course had some wide holes, like numbers six, eight, nine and even thirteen. But it also had some very narrow ones, such as ten and sixteen, or with trouble on only on one side, namely seventeen, eighteen, seven and two. The severity of number ten could have been a strong reason for reversing the nines. Playing out of its hundreds of trees along the entire length of that hole could mean a horrendous start for lots of golfers. The course had relatively small greens, especially compared to the mammoth putting surfaces on many recently constructed courses, often seen today on televised PGA tour events.

INDEX

A

Abbott, William 30
Aisel, Glenn 167, 171
Aladdin Country Club 24, 35
    hiring of Donald Ross 28
Albright, Bob 53
Alexander, Skip 146, 149
Allis, Percy 97
Altmaier, Elaine 30
Altmaier, John 28
    Dispatch cover 30
Altmaier, Mary K. 102
Altmaier, Oscar 86, 131
Amick, Bill
    American Society of Golf Course
        Architects, president of 175
    golfing at Wyandot 172
    junior golf at Wyandot 144
    observations of Lawrence Huber's
        greenkeeping methods 65
    return to Wyandot 175
    work with Lawrence Huber 69
Anderson, Paul 135
Arlington Country Club 54
Armour, Tommy 53, 54, 95

Arrow Sand and Gravel Company 22
Augusta National Golf Club 25, 134

B

Babcock, George 89
Balthaser, Dr. Fred 144, 172
Barnes, Jim 123
Bash Driving Range 119
Bash, Herb 119
Bauer, Alice 164
Bauer, Marlene 164
Beatty, Robert 42
Benevolent and Protective Order of Elks
    (BPOE) 18, 23, 27, 40, 81, 86
Berg, Patty 114
Bible, Harvey 68
Bishop, Glen
    article regarding course 98
    death 60
    Francis Marzolf, taught by 126
    Great Relay Race 116
    joins Wyandot Country Club 93
    1930 Ohio Amateur victory 55
    1931 Ohio Amateur performance 99
Boomer, Aubrey 97

Index

Braid, James 35
Brookside Golf and Country Club 59, 68, 80, 134, 136, 137, 154
   Charlie Lorms design of 45
Brown's Run Country Club 128
Buchanan, John
   marketing of Wyandot 167
   redesign of Wyandot course 169
   rerouting of holes 170
   Wyandot professional 166
Building Commission 156, 157, 159, 160, 164
Bulla, Johnny 146, 151
Burke, Billy 95, 98
Burke Golf Company 125
Byrer, Lew 57, 87, 112, 116

C

Campbell, James 28
Carmichael, Danny 146
Carpenter, Mel 60, 89, 146
Casparis Stone Company 21
Charity Newsies 22
Chiaverini, Val 169
Christo Rey Columbus High School 173
Ciuci, Henry 95
Claycraft Mining and Brick Company 22, 173
Cody, Bill 73
Colman, Ronald 52
Columbus Citizen 159
Columbus Citizen's Private Golf League 119
Columbus Coated Fabrics 22
Columbus Country Club 125, 145, 154
Columbus, Delaware & Marion Railway Company 46
Columbus District Golf Association 134, 143
Columbus Forge and Iron Company 69
Columbus Invitational 18
   complaints about rough 148
   PGA tour stop 145

Como, Perry 164
Cotton, Henry 97
Country Club of Buffalo 123
Cox, James 101
Cox, Wiffy 95
Crooks, F.S. 90
Crowe, Pat 118

D

Dawes, E. Cutler 53
Dean, Dizzy 164
Defense Homes Corporation 128
Delaware Country Club 35
Demaret, Jimmy 146, 164
Dempsey, Tom
   appointment as chair of organizing committee 86
   Great Relay Race 117
   Henry Watkins, rivalry with 87
   newspaper reference to 87
   Ohio Amateur, efforts to save 87
   organizing meeting, presentation to 86
   publicizing of improvements at Wyandot Country Club 89
   rakes in bunkers 90
   remarks on why Elks players do so well in championships 57
   success in retaining old Elks members 93
   Wyandot Country Club, recruitment of new members for 89
Deuschle, Bill 53, 54
   1928 Ohio Amateur winner 54
Deuschle, Martha 54, 60
Didrickson, Babe 46
Diegel, Leo 97
Donald J. Ross and Associates 32
Donald Ross Society 17
Downey, John 77, 79, 80
   selection as manager 30
Duncan, George 97
Dutcher, Don 117
Dutra, Olin 95
Dye, Pete 146

INDEX

E

Eagle, Chief Don 164
Edler, Shirley Aisel
  bus rides to Wyandot 166
  practice and play at Wyandot 166
  return to Wyandot 176
  Scioto Country Club champion 171
  South High golf team 166
  Wyandot, dreams of 172
Eickmeyer, F.C. 53
Elks Country Club 17
  challenges 17
  clubhouse, damage from fire 80
  Depression, coping with 77
  fire destroying clubhouse 79
  fourteenth hole design 39
  golf course dedication 39
  list of Ross courses 17
  member resignations in 1931 81
  1930 successes 77
  1931 disbanding of club 86
  1931 Ohio Amateur venue 77
  property footprint 51
  scorecard 47
Elson, Sally
  1935 Franklin County Amateur victory 113
  1937 Franklin County Amateur victory 113
  1937 Ohio Amateur victory 114
  Wyandot women's course record 113
  Wyandot women's star 112
Emmons, Mrs. Thornton (Isabel) 60, 77, 109, 110, 111, 112, 116
Evans, Chick 114

F

Fallis, Mrs. Linton 111
Favret, Rita (aka Rita Marzolf) 128
Ferrier, Jim 146
Fessenden, Paul 162
Finn, Karl 45

Finsterwald, Dow 126
Fisher, Dudley T., Jr.
  Skylarks cartoon 51
Florio, Johnny
  caddying 54
  death 60
  defeat in 1930 Ohio Amateur 55
  golf league all-star 120
  Great Relay Race 115
  1929 Ohio Amateur victory 55
  1931 Central Ohio Amateur victory 94
  1931 Ohio Amateur loss to James Reston 99
  1931 Ohio Amateur medalist in qualifying 99
  1932 Ohio Amateur victory 57
  Ohio State golf team 120
  resignation, consideration of 89
  shooting 64 137
  sports participation 54
  Wyandot Country Club, joining of 93
Fogle, Judge Wayne 146, 149
Ford, President Gerald 164
Frambes, Stark 57, 118
Franklin County Women's Golf Association 143

G

Glen Burn Company
  investment in course facilities in 1931 86
  John W. Kaufman's role as driving force 102
  members of partnership 86
  negotiations with the State of Ohio 137
  purchase of golf course from BPOE 85
  relationship with Wyandot Country Club 131
  sale of property to the State of Ohio 137
Godman Shoe Company 21
Golfdom magazine 126
Granville Golf Course 35

Index

Gullickson, Lloyd
  exhibition round at opening of course 41
  hitting ball off AIU Tower 46
  Inverness Country Club professional 46
  match with Ruth, Didrickson and Vare 46
  1922 U.S. Open performance 41
  Ohio Open victory in 1934 46
  performance at opening exhibition 45

H

Haas, Freddy 146
Hagen, Walter 54, 95, 97, 126
Hale America
  World War II golf events 136
Harbert, Chick 149
Hart, Eddie 89
Havers, Arthur 97
Hawkins, Fred 146
Hayes, Woody 101
Heafner, Clayton 146
Hedges, Hamilton 143
Heischman, Ray 137
Henderson, W.O. 43
Higgins, Charles 24
Higgins property 24
  description 27
  purchase 27
Hinchman, Bill 117
Hodson, Bert 97
Hogan, Ben 146
Holy, Dr. Thomas C. 156, 157, 158, 160
Hope, Bob 164
Hornung, Paul 143
Huber, Betty 61, 69
Huber, Bill 61
Huber, Bill, Sr. 69
Huber, Eunice
  courtship 63
  marriage 32
Huber, Jane 69

Huber, Jim 37, 61, 68, 69, 149, 153
Huber, Lawrence 31
  Brookside course improvements 68
  cartoon depiction 51
  contributions 65
  courtship of Eunice Daugherty 63
  death 69
  dissatisfaction of army's treatment of prisoners of war 68
  early life 61
  express messenger for Pennsylvania Railroad 63
  farming experience 37, 62
  fire destroying clubhouse, fighting of 78
  greenkeeper at Brookside 68
  hiring by The Elks 31
  interviewing for greenkeeper position 63
  invention of equipment 66
  involvement in greenkeepers' associations 63
  Marilyn Gohlke Strasser's rememberances of 63
  marriage 32, 63
  math ability 62
  observations of Donald Ross 37, 64
  orphanage stay 61
  preparing course for opening in 1923 40
  Purdue University agronomy course enrollment 66
  resignation from Wyandot 133
  retention as greenkeeper by Wyandot Country Club 87
  scientific method used in greenkeeping 65
  services as superintendent at Ohio State University golf courses 69
  tenure as greenkeeper 32
  World War II, service with U.S. Army Corps of Engineers 66
Hunt, Barney 146, 170
Hyatt, Shirley 69

Index

I

Independent Order of Odd Fellows 61
Indian Springs Golf Course 119, 137
Inverness Country Club 45, 46, 125

J

James Cox Trophy 98
Jilek, Byron 137
Jones, Bobby 25, 53, 97

K

Kaufman, Elizabeth Wagner 102
Kaufman, Harold
   death 173
   Glen Burn, role as member 86
   Glen Burn, role with 131
   golf committee chair 40
   involvement in opening course 40
   Marble Cliff Quarries involvement 24
   meeting with Donald Ross 35
   opening drive off number one hole 41
   receipt of plans from Ross 38
   speech at opening of course 42
   surviving son of John W. Kaufman 102
   Wyandot members, urging their purchase 131
Kaufman, John W. 27, 30
   acquisition of additional property 27
   acquisition of property for BPOE 26
   BPOE booster 23
   BPOE, passion for 102
   club memberships 22
   death 102
   early life 21
   heading up of building committee for Elks home 23
   home 24
   investment in course facilities in 1931 86
   investments 21
   involvement in opening course 40
   involvement with BPOE 22
   negotiations to buy property 27
   1925 western trip, return from 107
   positions in BPOE 23
   purchase of property, motivation for 85
   quarrying operations 22
   reaction to positive press accounts 45
   relationship with Donald Ross 33
   role in dedication of country home 28
   sale of club to Glen Burn, role 85
   services performed in obtaining country home of Elks 40
   speech at opening of course 42
   success of quarrying investments 33
   war chest drive 22
   western travel, love of 103
Kepler, Bob
   Columbus Invitational entry 146
   exhibition match participation opening Ohio State University golf courses 114
   golf coach of Jack Nicklaus at Ohio State 101
   1931 NCAA performance 94
   1931 Ohio Amateur defeat of Frank Lewis 99
   1931 Ohio Amateur finals match 100
Kessler, Kaye 76, 150, 172
KingTaste Products team 120
Kirby, Mary Kaufman 102
Kirkwood, Joe 126

L

Lafoon, Ky 146
Lake Forest Country Club 59, 91
La Moore, Mrs. Parker 114
Lausche, Governor Frank 162
Leatherlips 73
Lee, Raleigh W. 54, 56, 99
Legends of the Roving Brothers 103
Lewis, Frank 99
Little, Lawson 146, 164
Livesay, E.G. 116
Locke, Bobby 146

Index

Lorms, Bernadean Marzolf 124
Lorms, Charlie
  Francis Marzolf, hiring as assistant 124
  Francis Marzolf, relationship with 125
  golfing career 44
  marriage to Mary Dehner 125
  Mrs. Thornton Emmons, teaching of 109
  performance at opening exhibition match 45
  qualifying for U.S. Open 52
Lorms, Johnny 101, 128
Lynch, W.E. 94

M

MacDonald, Charles Blair 38
MacGregor Golf Company 127
Mack, Lathrop 56
Mangrum, Lloyd
  caddy tournament appearance 164
  Columbus Invitational, entry to 146
  Columbus Invitational victory at Wyandot 153
  complaints about rough at Wyandot 148
  Sunday battle with Schoux 152
Marble Cliff Quarry Co.
  changing of guard 42
  current status 173
  use of limestone in Columbus 21
Marchi, Al
  Aisel family friend 167
  Bonnie Randolph, teaching of 143
  hiring by Wyandot as its professional 141
  1947 Ohio Open victory 141
Margraf, Bill
  competition started by 118
  Marble Cliff Quarry experience 118
  marriage to and golf with Chester Skees 118
  Ohio Golf Association, executive secretary of 118
  singing voice 118

Margraf, Chester Skees
  1936 Franklin County Amateur performance 113
  1946 Franklin County Amateur victory 143
  Wyandot women's star 112
Marzolf, Clara 130
Marzolf, Edward 123
Marzolf, Ellen (aka Ellen Hallerman)
  gambling machine recollection 122
  golfing accomplishments for Ohio State women's team 128
  Ohio Statue University women's team player 114
Marzolf, Francis
  Arlington Country Club, professional at 125
  Brown's Run Country Club, professional at 128
  Burke Golf Company, designing clubs for 124
  Charlie Lorms, relationship with 125
  Columbus Invitational 146
  Columbus Invitational predictions 148
  description 123
  Elks Country Club, hiring as professional 77
  family of golf 123
  golf coach at Ohio State University 120
  golfing career 126
  Golf Professional of the Year 128
  Great Relay Race, setting up of 115
  MacGregor, club design work for 127
  Mrs. Thornton Emmons, evaluation of playing ability 109
  qualifying in 1928 U.S. Open 77
  resignation from Wyandot 133
  retention as professional by Wyandot Country Club 87
  shooting 64 137
  Teacher's Trophy victories in 1954 and 1955 126
  teaching philosophy 126
  teaching success 126

Index

World War II, work with Defense Homes Corporation 128
York Temple Country Club, professional at 128
Marzolf, Frank 128
Marzolf, Gene 124
Marzolf Machine 126
Marzolf, Martin 124
Marzolf, Mary Dehner 125
Marzolf, Ray 124
Marzolf, Tom 128
Matusoff, Max 89
McDermott, Johnny 123
McNutt, Paul 133
McVey, J.S. 91
Merion Golf Club 129
Middlecoff, Dr. Cary 146, 152
Midland Building 175
Miller, Ray 56
Moose, Bill
  background 71
  circus days 73
  death and funeral 74
  last of the Wyandots 76
  reasons for staying in Ohio 73
  resemblance to Wyandot's logo 87
  residence in shack south of Morse Road 72
  storyteller 76
Muldoon, Bill
  career in dentistry 171
  hole-in-one contest 170
  rivalry with Jack Nicklaus 170
Muldoon, Sam 170, 172

N

National Greenkeeper, The 65
Needham, Bill 87, 133
Needham, Russ 59, 118, 134, 137, 148, 154
Neil House Hotel 125
Nelson, Byron 46, 132, 146
Nelson, Mrs. Larry 111
Nicklaus, Jack 17, 101
Nieporte, Tom 101

O

Oakland Hills Country Club 125
Oakley, Annie 73
Odd Fellows' Home for Orphans 61
Ogilvie, Isabel 114
Ohio Federation of Organizations of the Deaf 156
Ohio Steel Foundry 22
Outhwaite, Joe 57, 99

P

Palmer, Johnny 146
Peniston, E.H. 41, 45, 89
Pennsylvania Railroad 63
PGA Championship of 1950 154
Pierce, George 79
Podolski, Bill 170
Portage Country Club 59
Powers, J.F. 86
Purdue University 126

R

Randolph, Bonnie 143
Ransick, Neil 55
Raymond, Bugs 119
Raymond Memorial Golf Course 143, 169
Redan hole design 38
Reinhard Bank 21
Remsick, Neil 55
Reston, James 99, 100, 101
Rhodes, Mayor James 17
  Columbus Invitational, efforts to secure Wyandot as venue of 146
  comments after Columbus Invitational 153
  compromise offer to Building Commission 161
  correspondence to State regarding saving Wyandot 156

Index

efforts to finad alternative location for schools 161
golf ability 164
offer to purchase Wyandot by City 156
plan to lease Wyandot as a municipal course 143
promotion of golf and caddies 163
reaction to House Finance Committee recommendation 159
receipt of Donald Ross award 164
showdown with Dale Stump at City hall 162
State Public Linx championship, Wyandot's holding of 144
strategy in trying to obtain Wyandot for the City 158
support of Buchanan's redesign effort 169
Wyandot municipal course, virtues of explained in correspondence 156
Wyandot, promotion of 144
Rhyan, Dick 166
Rohn, Glen 107
Ross, Alex 34
Ross, Donald 17
  Columbus visit 32
  courses designed 35
  decision to leave Scotland for United States 33
  design activities 33
  design of Aladdin 28
  Elks Country Club design characteristics 47
  Elks Country Club design plan 37
  Elks Country Club, observations of property 35
  importance of drainage 65
  meeting with golf committee 35
  playing career 33
  relationship with John W. Kaufman 33
  retention by BPOE 32
  staking of Elks Country Club 63
  visit to Elks Country Club 37

Royer-Price, Dick
  flag raising 41
Ruddy, Nelson 55
Ruth, Babe 46

S

Sarazen, Gene 41, 54, 95
Sargent, Alfred 54
Sargent, George
  coach of Ohio State University golf team 94
  golfing career 43
  leaving position as golf coach of Ohio State 120
  qualifying for U.S. Open 52
Schoux, George
  comments after tournament 153
  golf skill of 151
  penalty called 151
  professional from San Francisco 150
  Sunday battle with Mangrum 152
Scioto Country Club 154
Seidensticker, Norman 99
Sells Brothers Circus 73
Shannon, Arthur 35, 43
Shannon, Austin 99
Shaw, Representative Robert
  accused of conniving with Rhodes 162
  arguments to save Wyandot 158
  fishing trip 163
  House Finance Committee, arguments at 159
  sponsoring of bills to save Wyandot 158
Shute, Denny
  Brookside, controversy over leaving 91
  cartoon depiction 51
  club affiliations 59
  Columbus, reasons for leaving 92
  early pro career success 57
  election to World Golf Hall of Fame 60
  Hard Road farm 135
  inspector at Jeffrey Manufacturing 135
  match play success 58

INDEX

1927 U.S. Open performance 53
1930 Ohio Open victory 57
1931 U.S. Open performance 98
1933 Open Championship victory at St. Andrews 58
1936 and 1937 PGA Championship victories 58
1950 Ohio Open victory 59
1950 PGA Championship performance 59
playing in Columbus Golf League 135
Portage Country Club professional 60
Ryder Cup, foursomes match partnered with Walter Hagen 97
Ryder Cup of 1931, efforts to qualify for 91, 95
Ryder Cup, singles match victory 97
shoots Elks course record of 62 54
turns professional in 1928 53
victory in Central Ohio District Amateur 52
West Virginia Amateur victories 52
Shute, Hermon
Brookside, services as profesional at 92
Elks resignation 125
professional at Brookside 59
Simpson, Mrs. A.W. 114
Smith, Mrs. Hoyt 111
Snead, Sam 60, 146, 164
Sohl, Blanche
Ellen Marzolf, tutoring of 114
exhibition match participation opening Ohio State University golf courses 114
1931 Franklin County Amateur victory 109
1932 Franklin County Amateur performance 110
1936 Franklin County Amateur victory 113
Wyandot Country Club, joining of 112
Sohl, Curtis 94
Sohl, Pete 146
Springfield Country Club 35

State of Ohio Schools for the Deaf and Blind 18
building location 18, 51, 173
poor conditions at old school 159
sale of property for use of 137
St. John, L.W. 117, 120
Stranahan, Frank 146
Strasser, Marilyn Gohlke 63
Stump, Dale 156, 161, 163
Sullivan, Ed 164
Sumpter, Mrs. A. Ward 114

T

Taylor, T.V. 35, 43
Terango, Joanie 126
Thomas, James 42
Thomas, Joe 148
Thornton, Thornton 112
Timberlake, Ernest 78, 80
Todd, Harold 143
Tracewell, Allen 99
Trautman, George 115
Travis, Walter 123
Tufts, James 33
Twin Rivers Golf Course 143, 169

V

Vallette, Herb 44
Vare, Glenna Collett 46
victory gardens
Columbus golf clubs planting of 136
Vines, Ellsworth 146
Von Elm, George 98

W

Walsh, Frank 95
Walters, Dr. John 79
Washburn, Representative L.C. 162
Watkins, Cy 120, 131
Watkins, Dwight 47, 60, 120, 131, 172, 176
Watkins, Henry
appointment as member 86

INDEX

Watkins Printing Company 120
Weber, Harold 54
Whipp, Frank 87
Winding Hollow Country Club 45
Wood, Craig 59, 95, 126
Woodruff and Pausch Company 21
World War II
  draft 133
  golf clubs affected by 132
  golf course maintenance, consequences of discontinuing 133
  golfers, derision faced during 134
  public support 132
  rationing of automobile tires 132
  rationing of gasoline 132
Worsham, Lew 146
Wyandot Country Club 17
  challenges 17
  changes in operation 93
  college functions at 122
  description by Russ Needham 138
  description of club and course 60
  disbanding of in 1946 143
  gambling at 122
  Great Relay Race, publicity caused by 117
  John W. Kaufman's role in establishing 102
  membership, terms and conditions 86
  members, predicament of by imminent closing of course 141
  name change 18
  naming 87
  1931 Ohio Amateur, fears regarding shortness of course 98
  1931 Ohio Amateur qualifying rounds 98
  1931 Ohio Amateur, success of members in qualifying 99
  1946 Franklin County Women's Amateur, hosting of 143
  Ohio Amateur of 1931, securing 90
  rationing, response to 132

Scioto Country Club, defeat of in team competition 93
Victory Garden 136
World War II, efforts to keep operating during 134
World War II, efforts to raise revenue during 135
World War II golfing achievements 136
Wyandot Golf Course-Centerburg 17
Wyandot municipal course
  demolition begins 164
  junior memberships 144
  lease from the State of Ohio 144
  1951 Columbus Public Links Championship, hosting of 170
  patronage by public course players 144

Y

York Temple Country Club 24, 59, 80, 128, 137

Z

Zanesville Country Club 137
Zooligans
  Columbus Invitational prize money 146
  preparation for 1948 Columbus Invitational 146
  sponsor of Columbus Invitational 145

About the Author

Bill Case is a retired Columbus, Ohio litigation attorney. His love of golf and appreciation for its history and courses has launched him into researching and writing about the game. As a member of the Donald Ross Society, Bill has a special interest in preserving Ross's work, as well as the memory of his "lost" courses. Bill and his wife, Lisa, split their time between Columbus, Scotland and Ross's home of Pinehurst, golfing at all three locales whenever possible. His daughter, Hadley, is also a writer in Miami Beach.

Visit us at
www.historypress.net

This title is also available as an e-book

www.ingramcontent.com/pod-product-compliance
Lightning Source LLC
Chambersburg PA
CBHW060758100426
42813CB00004B/868